THE MAGICAL WORLDS OF NARNIA

THE MAGICAL WORLDS OF NARNIA

A TREASURY OF MYTHS AND LEGENDS

DAVID COLBERT

PUFFIN

PUFFIN BOOKS

Published by the Penguin Group
Penguin Books Ltd, 80 Strand, London WC2R 0RL, England
Penguin Group (USA) Inc., 375 Hudson Street, New York, New York 10014, USA
Penguin Group (Canada), 90 Eglinton Avenue East, Suite 700, Toronto, Ontario, Canada
M4P 2Y3 (a division of Pearson Penguin Canada Inc.)
Penguin Ireland, 25 St Stephen's Green, Dublin 2, Ireland
(a division of Penguin Books Ltd)
Penguin Group (Australia), 250 Camberwell Road, Camberwell, Victoria 3124, Australia
(a division of Pearson Australia Group Pty Ltd)
Penguin Books India Pvt Ltd, 11 Community Centre, Panchsheel Park,
New Delhi – 110 017, India
Penguin Group (NZ), cnr Airborne and Rosedale Roads, Albany, Auckland 1310, New
Zealand (a division of Pearson New Zealand Ltd)
Penguin Books (South Africa) (Pty) Ltd, 24 Sturdee Avenue, Rosebank, Johannesburg
2196, South Africa

Penguin Books Ltd, Registered Offices: 80 Strand, London WC2R 0RL, England

www.penguin.com

First published 2005
2

Copyright © David Colbert, 2005

The moral right of the author has been asserted

Set in Adobe Garamond

Made and printed in England by Clays Ltd, St Ives plc

British Library Cataloguing in Publication Data
A CIP catalogue record for this book is available from the British Library

ISBN-13: 978-0-14131-994-0
ISBN-10: 0-14131-994-1

Thanks to
Liz Katz and Clare Hulton
for their hard work and many thoughtful contributions.

'. . . a man writing a story is too excited about the story itself to sit back and notice how he is doing it . . .'

– C. S. Lewis, 'It All Began with a Picture'

CONTENTS

Abbreviations of book titles:

The Chronicles of Narnia:

The Lion, the Witch and the Wardrobe: LWW

The Magician's Nephew: MN

The Horse and His Boy: HHB

Prince Caspian: PC

The Voyage of the 'Dawn Treader': VDT

The Silver Chair: SC

The Last Battle: LB

Other books by Lewis:

Boxen: The Imaginary World of the Young C. S. Lewis

Surprised by Joy

The Abolition of Man

Letters to Children

Letters of C. S. Lewis

The Collected Letters of C. S. Lewis, Volume 1

The Collected Letters of C. S. Lewis, Volume 2

God in the Dock

Miracles

That Hideous Strength

The Essential C. S. Lewis

The Pilgrim's Regress

Reflections on the Psalms

Christian Reflections

Mere Christianity

The World's Last Night

Books about Lewis:

C. S. Lewis: A Companion and Guide,
by Walter Hooper

C. S. Lewis: A Biography, by Roger Lancelyn Green
and Walter Hooper

INTRODUCTION

Many people hear about Narnia without learning it has what C. S. Lewis called a 'hidden story'. After reading *The Lion, the Witch and the Wardrobe*, or seeing one of its many film adaptations, they may be told the big secret. A brother or sister or friend says, 'Could you tell it was all about God?' But for anyone who looks into it, there's another surprise to follow: the big secret is wrong. The *Chronicles* are not all about God. They're about medieval literature, and British politics, and inside jokes and a long list of other things, the most important of which is C. S. Lewis himself.

The older sister who gave me the *Chronicles* didn't mention religion until I had finished the first six books. Although I'd recognized some of it in *The Lion, the Witch and the Wardrobe*, I'd missed all the rest. That's exactly what Lewis intended. He wanted readers to be so caught up in the story that they don't think about what they're reading. Instead he wanted them to feel it, to experience religion as an emotion rather than an idea.

The fairy-tale animals and witches of Narnia are more than calculated ploys to make the Bible more appealing. Lewis believed fairy tales and religion were naturally connected. He saw myths and legends as a step in humankind's development of belief. To him, they were part of a logical path to Christianity. When lecturing his university students about the medieval epic poem *The Faerie Queene* (1590), by Edmund Spenser, he said: 'Anywhere in this wood . . . you may hear angels singing – or come upon satyrs romping. What is more, the satyrs may lead you to the angels' (*Spenser's Images of Life*, p.96). A faun – Roman mythology's version of the satyr in Greek myths – appears in the very first chapter of *The Lion, the Witch and the Wardrobe*. Lucy Pevensie comes upon him, and by the end of the book the Pevensies are led to the angels.

Lewis didn't mind that the path through paganism was muddy. The novelist and critic Penelope Fitzgerald, who attended Lewis's Oxford lectures, once recalled the pencil notes she made in her copy of Spenser: 'CSL says forget court- ly Spenser dreamy Spenser – think of rustic Spenser English Spenser homely Spenser, kindled lust, worldly muck, bagpipes and goat-milking.' Worldly muck. No, Narnia is not just about God.

When Lewis wrote the *Chronicles* he was in his fifties and had been thinking about this blend of profane and sacred for a long time. The faun that Lucy meets, Mr Tumnus, had been in Lewis's head since Lewis was sixteen. Lewis once said that a mental picture of Tumnus, 'carrying an umbrella and parcels in a snowy wood', was a starting point for the *Chronicles*. (*Of Other Worlds,* p.42) He meant this to explain that the books weren't overtly Christian when he first imagined them. But as Lewis himself warned, 'You must not believe all that authors tell you about how they write their books . . . When the story is finished, he has forgotten a good deal of what writing it was like.' Lewis didn't really draw a line between Mr Tumnus and Aslan. That's why both are in Narnia. Mixing pagan religion and fairy tales with the gospels was in Lewis's nature. There's no way Lewis, in his fifties, could have set pen to paper and not written about religion.

Although Narnia is rooted in personal fantasy, it grew from something real. Just before the beginning of the Second World War, in September 1939, Lewis and his companion welcomed to their home in Oxford four children who had been sent there from London to avoid enemy air attacks. Shortly afterwards Lewis jotted down a few lines of an idea that was forming:

> This book is about four children whose names were Ann, Martin, Rose and Peter . . . They all had to go away from London suddenly because of the Air Raids . . . They were sent to stay with a relation of Mother's who was a very old Professor who lived by himself in the country. (*C. S. Lewis: A Companion and Guide*, 402)

Nearly ten years later, that paragraph, a little shorter and with different names, became the beginning of the *The Lion, the Witch and the Wardrobe*.

The original plan was modest. Lewis wasn't thinking of even one sequel when he started the story. As John Clute and John Grant say in their insightful and witty *Encyclopedia of Fantasy*, '*The Lion, the Witch and the Wardrobe* was clearly written in haste, beginning as a romp.' As a result, when you read the *Chronicles* you get both *Deus* and *deus ex machina* — both God and the god in the machine, the narrative leaps that take a writer over the sticky spots. Perhaps for that reason, Lewis's friends weren't wholeheartedly encouraging. One, J. R. R. Tolkien, didn't like the way Lewis threw together elements from so many different traditions without trying to unify them. Tolkien's appraisal was, 'It really won't do, you know!' He would have tried to make the pieces fit together before showing it to anyone. Tolkien wasn't the only friend who raised an eyebrow. Roger Lancelyn Green, later a Lewis biographer, read an early draft and questioned, among other things, the sudden and brief appearance of Father Christmas. He felt it broke the magic. He didn't think it was consistent with what happened earlier in the book.

Lewis disagreed. He forgave stories without beautiful structures. He once defended Spenser's *Faerie Queene* against the same criticism by talking about the poem as a parade, a 'pageant' of symbols, one after another. We 'simpletons', he said, are meant to watch the show as it goes by (*Spenser's Images of Life*, p.2). It was no great leap for him to insist a good Christmas parade must end with Father Christmas.

The same goes for the structure of Lewis's ideas. They don't all fit together. They fit with some parts of his life even less. Forcing them doesn't work. In some cases that's just because he's human. In others, it's because Lewis died before he had a chance to edit the *Chronicles* and remove inconsistencies, which he'd been planning to do.

Whether the pieces fit smoothly or rub so hard they break doesn't matter to me. Either way, what's interesting is which pieces Lewis chose, and why he tried to make them mesh. Many of the elements in the *Chronicles* came from parts of his history and personality that Lewis didn't fully understand or acknowledge. Others he did understand, but only after experiencing them as confusing feelings. Some were things he was trying to resolve for himself. He wasn't always successful. That's how it is with feelings; and feelings, more than ideas, are what the *Chronicles* are about.

The *Chronicles* have a hold on readers that lasts long past childhood. They capture something explained by Robert Louis Stevenson, one of the authors whose so-called children's books had a similar hold on Lewis: 'Stories may be nourished with the realities of life, but their true mark is to satisfy the nameless longings of the reader'.

Nameless longings. That sums up exactly what Lewis wanted readers to experience in the *Chronicles*. It's what drove him to create Narnia. This book attempts to give some of those longings a name.

THE LION, THE WITCH AND THE WARDROBE: LEWIS'S THOUGHTS

There's a story – only possibly true, but told often – that when Walter Hooper, a Lewis biographer and editor, asked Lewis about the name 'Narnia', Lewis showed him a book from his childhood titled *Murray's Small Classical Atlas*. Within it, on a map of Italy, Lewis had underlined the name of a little town with that name. Now known as Narni, the town sits at the top of a hill near the very centre of Italy.

If Lewis didn't make note of the name during childhood, he probably first read about the town in an old Latin text. Paul F. Ford, author of *Companion to Narnia*, counts at least seven references to the small town by Roman authors such as Livy, Pliny the Elder and Pliny the Younger.

However, it was Ireland, where Lewis was born, that first inspired him to start writing. As a small boy, Lewis lived in a large house in

Lewis dedicated the first Narnia book to his god-daughter, Lucy Barfield. The character Lucy Pevensie was also named after her.

In Roman
mythology,
Vertumnus is a
god who rules
the seasons and
plant life. His
great love was
Pomona, the
nymph who was
patron of the
fruit orchards,
especially
apples.

Mr Tumnus is
very pleased to
meet Lucy,
whom he calls a
'Daughter of
Eve', after
another apple
lover.

the countryside with his elder brother, Warren, and his parents. In his memoir, *Surprised by Joy*, he says that because it was often rainy there, he and his brother Warren spent much of their time inside, imagining the world beyond their windows. Their curiosity and frustration led each of them to invent make-believe worlds. Lewis called his 'Animal-Land'. Warren was more interested in trains and steam ships. His world was an imaginary version of India, then a British colony.

Lewis and Warren brought the two worlds together with a series of maps, routes and characters to create the kingdom of Boxen. Many of the characters in these worlds were talking animals and animal knights. If you want to find the earliest signs of what would become the chivalrous mouse Reepicheep of Narnia, look at the earliest Boxen story, *The King's Ring*, which introduced Sir Peter Mouse, a knight 'in waiting on the King' (*Boxen*, p.25).

Lewis spent a lot of time working on the Boxen stories while Warren was away at school, developing 700 years of Boxen history in the process. In a letter, eight-year-old Lewis wrote to his twelve-year-old brother, 'I am thinking of writeing a History of Mouse-land . . . Mouse-land had a very long stone-age . . .

it lasted from 55 BC to 1212 and then king Bublich I began to reign . . . Bub II his son fought indai about the lantern act, died 1377 king Bunny came next' (*Boxen*, p.10).

AN UNCOWARDLY LION

It's easy for us now, so many years after the *Chronicles* were published, to assume a direct connection between 'Animal-Land' and 'Aslan'. The second name even seems to be an unconscious echo of the first. But for Lewis the worlds were different. Unlike the *Chronicles*, some of the Boxen plots are focused on political battles, apparently reflecting the interests of Lewis's parents. From the start Lewis had different ideas about Narnia. However, he didn't have a plot. 'At first I had very little idea how the story would go,' he said. 'But then suddenly Aslan came bounding into it' (*Of Other Worlds*, p.42).

Talk about a welcome guest.

The combination of Aslan and the faun Mr Tumnus sums up the appeal of Narnia. Mr Tumnus comes from the rollicking world of classical myths, the same tradition that brought to Narnia dryads and nymphs and mischievous Bacchus. Tumnus is a pagan figure from the nature worship that Christianity displaced. Aslan is Jesus in fur.

The full title of the Boxen stories is *Boxen: Or Scenes from Boxonian City Life*.

A psychologist would be amused to learn that a man who in many ways was stuck in childhood had created a 'Boxonian' world as a child and then lived most of his adult life in Oxford – making him an 'Oxonian'.

'Aslan' is the
Turkish word for
'lion'. Lewis
said he found
the name in an
edition of *The
Arabian Nights.*
In *Companion to
Narnia*, Paul F.
Ford notes that
'As' is the
Scandinavian
word for God.
Lewis had been
in love with
Norse tales
about Asgard,
the home of the
gods, since he
was a young
teenager. He
and fellow
Oxford professor
J. R. R. Tolkien
had a club that
met to read and
discuss those
legends. (See
p.68.)

Still, they aren't such an unlikely pair. Along with the work of writers like Spenser – whose satyrs could lead to angels – Lewis would have known about stories like the Anglo-Saxon epic *Beowulf,* which combines the pagan and Christian worlds brilliantly.

There's also nothing unusual about Christ taking the form of a lion. It's an old symbol, like the lamb and the unicorn. Jesus is referred to as the 'Lion of the tribe of Judah' in the Bible (Revelations 5:5). However, it wasn't a conscious choice. 'I think I had been having a good many dreams of lions about that time,' Lewis tried to explain. 'Apart from that, I don't know where the Lion came from or why He came. But once He was there He pulled the whole story together, and soon He pulled the six other Narnia stories in after Him' (*Of Other Worlds,* p.42). (Lewis sometimes capitalized the 'H' when referring to Aslan as 'He', as if he were writing about God.)

Despite the symbolism of Aslan's character, Lewis doesn't follow the Bible exactly. *The Lion, the Witch and the Wardrobe* isn't an allegory – there's no simple, one-to-one symbolic relationship between things or people inside the story and ideas outside of it. Lewis had written an allegory before. It wasn't his most interesting book. He knew something like it wouldn't appeal to younger readers. More importantly, it wouldn't appeal to him. As he put it to a young reader, in the *Chronicles* he wanted to show what *might* have happened if Christ had lived in Narnia. The events are 'like those in our world, but not exactly like'. The term he used for this was 'supposal', as in, 'Suppose this happened . . .'

In other words, Aslan always does what Jesus would do; but he doesn't always do what Jesus did.

Lewis's early allegory was *The Pilgrim's Regress* (1933), his first work of prose. (He had published poetry earlier.) It's about a man who runs from religion, then returns to it.

The title comes from John Bunyan's *The Pilgrim's Progress* (1678), a famous religious work about a man who makes his way to 'the Celestial City', heaven.

WHY A WARDROBE?

Lion, witch . . . *wardrobe*? It's as if the title slipped on a banana peel. First, two grand images of fantasy and dangerous adventure; then, plop, a piece of old furniture. Why does a world as colourful as Narnia have such a humdrum entrance?

There are two reasons, both from Lewis's childhood.

THERE'S NO PLACE LIKE HOME

When Lewis was seven, his family moved to a new, large home. In his memoir, *Surprised by Joy*, he says that house:

> is almost a major character in my [life] story. I am a product of long corridors, empty sunlit rooms, upstairs indoor silences, attics explored in solitude, distant noises of gurgling cisterns and pipes, and

Philip Pullman, who has often criticized Lewis, and whose books turn many of Lewis's ideas upside down, began the first volume of the *His Dark Materials* series with a child hiding in a wardrobe. He didn't realize the ironic connection until later.

25

the noise of wind under the tiles. (*Surprised by Joy*, p.10)

This house was like the Professor's house which the Pevensies explore: 'the sort of house that you never seem to come to the end of . . . full of unexpected places' (*The Lion, the Witch and the Wardrobe*, ch.1).

In Lewis's home was a wardrobe that his grandfather had made for him – and which, according to his brother, Warren, was the inspiration for the title of the first of the *Chronicles*. That wardrobe is now on display at Wheaton College in Illinois.

'ONE NOTABLE EXCEPTION'

Life would be easy for Lewis biographers if Lewis had played inside that wardrobe. No such luck. In fact, Douglas Gresham, Lewis's stepson, even disagrees with Warren. He says no particular wardrobe inspired Lewis. He may be right, if you count only real ones. The connection to an imaginary wardrobe was spotted by Lewis biographers long ago.

What most fascinated Lewis about the house were its 'endless books'. They were everywhere. All kinds of books. 'In the seemingly endless rainy afternoons,' he said, 'I took volume after volume from the shelves' (*Surprised by Joy*, p.10).

Along with the wardrobe from Lewis's childhood, Wheaton College's Wade Centre is home to items like Lewis's desk and pipe, as well as 2,300 of his letters, 2,400 books from his library and childhood photos.

Lewis quickly jumped from nursery rhymes and fairy tales to longer adventure stories. 'The one notable exception,' however, according to biographers Walter Hooper and Roger Lancelyn Green, was the work of Edith Nesbit.

E. Nesbit (1858–1924) – as an author she was known by her first initial, not her full name – was one of Britain's most popular authors during Lewis's childhood. Some of her books, such as *The Railway Children* (1906), are still favourites.

Lewis was one of those readers who loved Nesbit's books even as an adult. Lewis didn't discover some of Nesbit's many stories until he was in his twenties. He didn't hesitate to read ones he'd missed, even though he was well on his way to a career as a serious academic. When he was twenty-four years old he noted in his diary, 'I dreamed that in a station waiting room I found a children's story which I had never seen before, by E. Nesbit; and became so interested that I missed my train' (*C. S. Lewis: A Biography*, p.236).

More than two decades later, while working on *The Lion, the Witch and the Wardrobe*, Lewis explained the project to a critic by saying he was finishing a children's book 'in the tradition of E. Nesbit'. Anyone back then

We don't learn that Susan, Peter, Lucy and Edmund's surname is Pevensie until *The Voyage of the 'Dawn Treader'*. No one knows what inspired it, but given Lewis's interest in medieval history, it could have come from the town of Pevensey on the English coast. That's where the French duke who would become William the Conquerer, King of England, landed with his troops.

would have understood he meant a story about a family of children having an unlikely, magical adventure. Nesbit wrote many such books.

Readers of Nesbit's books may notice a similarity of style in the *Chronicles* – not just the narrator's voice, but also the way the characters speak. Biographer A.N. Wilson puts it: 'They are E. Nesbit children; they "jaw" rather than talk; they say "by gum!" and "Crikey!"'

There are also many similarities in their stories. As Professor Mervyn Nicholson puts it, 'The extent of Lewis' borrowing from Nesbit is remarkable, drawing [not only] precise details but also plot configurations and character types from Nesbit for his own creations.' Several scholars have noted this. (Nicholson isn't troubled by it. Some are, though no one can say Lewis fails to make something new of Nesbit's material.)

There isn't room here to list every similarity. Several come up in the chapters that follow. As you'll discover, they run from the beginning of the *Chronicles* to the end. And by beginning, I mean the wardrobe.

One Nesbit story with a familiar ring for fans of the *Chronicles* is called 'The Aunt and Amabel'. The story begins when young Amabel gets into trouble and is banished to

At the beginning of *The Magician's Nephew*, Lewis says the story is set when 'Mr Sherlock Holmes was still living in Baker Street and the Bastables were looking for treasure in the Lewisham Road'. The Bastables were a fictional family Nesbit introduced in *The Story of the Treasure Seekers* (1899).

her aunt's guest room, 'the one with the four-post bed and the red curtains and the large wardrobe with a looking-glass [mirror] in it'. In *The Lion, the Witch and the Wardrobe*, the Pevensie children 'looked into a room that was quite empty except for one big wardrobe; the sort that has a looking-glass in the door' (*The Lion, the Witch and the Wardrobe*, ch.1).

In the Nesbit story, Amabel looks for something to read and all she can find is 'one book covered in red velvet'. It turns out to be a train timetable. As she skims through it she sees the destination name 'Whereyouwanttogoto'. And then: 'The name of the station was "Bigwardrobeinspareroom".'

It seems that Lewis's dream about stepping into a Nesbit railway station really *was* a trip through a wardrobe he remembered.

Nesbit's Amabel opens the wardrobe door and steps inside, only to find 'most amazingly, a crystal cave, very oddly shaped like a railway station. It seemed to be lighted by stars, which is, of course, unusual in a booking office, and over the station clock was a full moon'. In *The Lion, the Witch and the Wardobe*, Lucy Pevensie also steps into an unusual night scene, and is drawn by a light to the lamp-post where she meets Mr Tumnus.

Crikey!

Nesbit and her husband, Hubert Bland, helped found the Fabian Society, a progressive political group that became the basis for Britain's Labour Party. It's still an important part of British political life.

The Fabian Society is also one of the sources of J. K. Rowling's fictional 'Order of the Phoenix'. She has used names of its real founders to make names for members of the Order.

The Snow Queen and Kay, from
Hans Christian Andersen's 'The Snow Queen'.

HOW DID LEWIS MAKE HELL FREEZE OVER?

LWW:
Jadis, the
White Witch

The Pevensie children think the White Witch, Jadis, is two-faced – nice when she wants to trap Edmund, cruel as soon as she has done the deed. They're nowhere near the truth. Five-faced is more like it.

Lewis invented Jadis from several unusual sources. Her iciness, her pretension, her anger, her destructiveness, her ambition to rule Narnia – all these come from literary characters Lewis knew well.

COLD, COLD HEART

Lewis said the character of Jadis came to him as an imaginary picture, as Mr Tumnus and Aslan did. In his mind he saw 'a queen on a sledge'. That's how she makes her first appearance in *The Lion, the Witch and the Wardrobe*: in a sledge pulled by two reindeer. 'I don't know where the pictures came from,' Lewis said many years later, when he was asked

The name 'Jadis' is used only once in *The Lion, the Witch and the Wardrobe* – in the notice pinned to Mr Tumnus's door – but the White Witch and Jadis are one and the same.

Lewis knew the word 'Jadis' from a medieval French poem, 'Ballade des Dames du Temps Jadis' ('Ballad of the Ladies of Days Gone By'), by Francois Villon (1431–85).

The poem is a lament for women like the Greek nymph Echo and Joan of Arc. It mentions a Queen Blanche – a White Queen – and its famous refrain is 'Ou sont les neiges d'antan?' ('Where are the snows of yesteryear?')

how he came to write Narnia (*Of Other Worlds*, p.42).

This may be one of those times when, as Lewis said, an author has forgotten how a book came to be. That first image of Jadis is practically identical to the title character in Hans Christian Andersen's fairy tale, 'The Snow Queen'. Andersen's Snow Queen tempts a young boy to give in to evil, then takes him to a cold, empty place, just as Lewis's White Witch does. Both *The Lion, the Witch and the Wardrobe* and Andersen's fairy tale are about evil in the soul and how to defeat it.

In 'The Snow Queen', the evil is created by a devilish hobgoblin: 'He made a looking-glass which had the power of making everything good or beautiful that was reflected in it almost shrink to nothing, while everything that was worthless and bad looked increased in size and worse than ever.' When the looking-glass is shattered high in the sky, tiny shards of it enter the hearts of some people. They don't feel the wound, but it distorts their characters, making them love things they shouldn't. The same happens to the eyes of some unlucky people, distorting appearances. What should look bad looks good. When shards distort the eyes and the heart of a young boy named Kay, he falls prey to the Snow Queen, just as

Edmund fell for the White Witch in Narnia:

... [A] great sledge came by; it was painted white, and in it sat someone wrapped in a rough white fur and wearing a white cap. The sledge drove twice round the square, and Kay fastened his own little sledge to it, so that when it went away, he followed with it. It went faster and faster right through the next street, and then the person who drove turned round and nodded pleasantly to Kay, just as if they were acquainted with each other, but whenever Kay wished to loosen his little sledge the driver nodded again, so Kay sat still, and they drove out through the town gate. Then the snow began to fall so heavily that the little boy could not see a hand's breadth before him, but still they drove on; then he suddenly loosened the cord so that the large sledge might go on without him, but it was of no use, his little carriage held fast, and away they went like the wind. ... The boy was frightened, and tried to say a prayer, but he could remember nothing but the multiplication table.

... All at once they sprang on one side, the great sledge stopped, and the

In 'The Quest of Belheris', an unfinished work Lewis wrote as a teenager, a man named Wan Jadis appears. He is searching for 'the land of Yesterday' where 'the queens of olden song abide, Helen, Isolde and Guinevere, deathless forever in their sorrow and loveliness'.

person who had driven it rose up. The fur and the cap, which were made entirely of snow, fell off, and he saw a lady, tall and white. It was the Snow Queen.

'We have driven well,' said she, 'but why do you tremble? Here, creep into my warm fur.' Then she seated him beside her in the sledge, and as she wrapped the fur round him he felt as if he were sinking into a snow drift.

'Are you still cold?' she asked, as she kissed him on the forehead. The kiss was colder than ice; it went quite through to his heart, which was already almost a lump of ice; he felt as if he were going to die, but only for a moment; he soon seemed quite well again, and did not notice the cold around him.

Lewis once referred to Jadis as a 'Circe' character, from the sorceress in Homer's *The Odyssey* who turns Odysseus's men into pigs. (See also 15.)

Trusting the Snow Queen is a serious mistake for Kay. The looking-glass shards are to blame. They make Kay believe that cold is good, even when the Queen keeps him in her castle near the North Pole, where he 'sleeps at her feet' for so long that almost everyone thinks he is dead.

A lot of trouble could have been avoided if Edmund had read this fairy tale. Here's what Jadis says after first discovering Edmund in snowy Narnia and learning he is a human boy – just what she needs, as Queen of Narnia, to defeat Aslan:

> 'My poor child,' she said in a quite different voice, 'how cold you look! Come and sit with me here on the sledge . . .'
>
> Edmund did not like this arrangement at all but he dared not disobey; he stepped onto the sledge and sat at her feet, and she put a fold of her fur mantle round him and tucked it well in. (*The Lion, the Witch and the Wardrobe*, ch.4)

Andersen's Kay and Lewis's Edmund are interchangeable. Just as the Snow Queen takes advantage of the evil that struck Kay in the form of glass shards, the White Witch plays on the moral weaknesses and distorted view of the world that are inside Edmund because Edmund inherited sin from Adam and Eve.

Fortunately for Kay, his friend Gerda refuses to give up on him, and sets out to find him. Soon she hears about the Snow Queen, and learns about the Queen's castle from a reindeer who comes from the far north. (Remember the reindeer pulling Jadis's sled?) Gerda finds Kay there, and, because her heart is filled with Christian love, she is able to help

The Snow Queen in the Andersen story enjoys creating an eternal winter wherever she goes, just like Jadis, 'who has made a magic so that it is always winter in Narnia' (*The Lion, the Witch and the Wardrobe*, ch.4).

dislodge the evil shard. The same kind of love saves Edmund in *The Lion, the Witch and the Wardrobe*.

Where did Lewis's mysterious image of the queen on a sled come from? No mystery there.

THE BABBLIN' QUEEN

One of the funniest scenes of the *Chronicles* occurs in *The Magician's Nephew*, when Jadis appears in London. Lewis borrowed it from an E. Nesbit tale, *The Story of the Amulet*. In Nesbit's version, the Queen of ancient Babylon magically appears in modern London to visit the book's young heroes, whom she has met earlier. Chaos follows.

> 'Good gracious!' cried Anthea, 'what's that?' The loud hum of many voices came through the open window. Words could be distinguished . . .
>
> Then came a clear voice that they knew.
>
> 'Retire, slaves!' it said.
>
> 'What's she a saying of?' cried a dozen voices. 'Some blamed foreign lingo,' one voice replied.
>
> The children rushed to the door. A crowd was on the road and pavement.

Novelist Joan D. Vinge won the distinguished Hugo Award for her modern retelling of the Andersen story, also entitled *The Snow Queen*.

In the middle of the crowd, plainly to be seen from the top of the steps, were the beautiful face and bright veil of the Babylonian Queen.

'Jimminy!' cried Robert, and ran down the steps, 'here she is!'

. . . The crowd was all talking at once, and getting rather angry. But no one seemed to think of blaming the Queen.

. . . 'We shall have the police here directly,' said Anthea in the tones of despair . . .

Anthea doesn't need to worry. Although a constable does arrive in Lewis's version, in the Nesbit story the children take the Queen to the British Museum. Unfortunately, just as Jadis robbed a shop to get 'jewels . . . fit for my rank' (*The Magician's Nephew*, ch.6), Nesbit's Queen of Babylon tries to take the 'necklaces and earrings and things' from the cases at the Museum. (In the Queen's defence, the jewels *were* hers a few thousand years earlier.)

JADIS-WHO-MUST-BE-OBEYED
The angry side of Jadis's character comes directly from another favourite author of Lewis. Sir Henry Rider Haggard (1856–1925)

Andersen wrote another story like 'The Snow Queen'. Called 'The Ice Maiden', it doesn't end as happily. Jackie Wullschlager, a biographer of Hans Christian Andersen, says the stories are 'rooted in Andersen's early life'. When Andersen was eleven his father died, and his mother told him, 'The Ice Maiden has carried him off.'

was a bestselling author during Lewis's childhood. His adventure stories aren't read widely now, but some, like *King Solomon's Mines* and *Allan Quatermain and the Lost City of Gold*, still inspire movies.

As with Nesbit, echoes of Haggard's influence can be seen in many of Lewis's themes, settings, plot elements and characters. Jadis is one of the most obvious. Professor Mervyn Nicholson says 'Jadis owes more to Haggard than she does to Nesbit: Lewis adapted Nesbit's plot to his purpose, fusing it with Haggard's characterization.' Jadis, as Nicholson explains, comes from Haggard's character Ayesha, also known as She and She-Who-Must-Be-Obeyed. Ayesha appeared in a series of novels, starting with *She: A Story of Adventure* (1886). A goddess, she rules a lost world discovered by the hero of the book.

Like Jadis, Ayesha is arrogant, seductive and cruel. Other characters are both attracted to her and repulsed by her at the same time, a strange combination of feelings that Edmund experiences in *The Lion, the Witch and the Wardrobe.*

As Nicholson points out, Jadis snaps at her underlings, just as Ayesha does. She literally 'blasts' through locked doors, as Ayesha does. And most important, Jadis fights a rebellion

Haggard was one of the first authors to have a book turned into a movie. His novel *She* was filmed in 1899, during the earliest days of cinema. It has been remade at least nine times since, most recently in 2001. *King Solomon's Mines* has also been filmed many times, most recently in 2004.

led by her sister, just as Ayesha fights a love rival she considers to be a kind of sister. Both rebellions end with similar declarations of triumph. When Jadis's sister makes the mistake of claiming victory too soon, Jadis says, 'Yes . . . Victory, but not yours" (*The Magician's Nephew*, ch.5). In the Haggard novel, Ayesha says to her sisterly rival, 'Think not that I am conquered, for my name now is Victory!'

THE EVE OF DESTRUCTION

As if Ayesha isn't enough of a villain to use as a model, Lewis found another source for Jadis in a story connected to the Bible.

Mr Beaver mentions her to the Pevensies. Jadis, he explains, is the daughter of Lilith, 'your father Adam's first wife' (*The Lion, the Witch and the Wardrobe*, ch.8). There's a lot of history behind that remark.

In the myths of ancient Mesopotamia, Lilith was a demon who seduced men and stole children. Her story survives on the edges of the Jewish and Christian traditions. By now it's difficult to distinguish between the strands of the story that are traditional and those woven in by later writers.

The story Mr Beaver mentions is one of those later inventions. It's based on a vague

Fantasy fiction experts John Clute and John Grant say Haggard 'could slip from subtlety to coarseness, from original insight to tendentious cliché within a single paragraph'. They add, 'there is almost always a lingering sense that [a Haggard] tale could be told better. Over the past century, many writers have tried to do this.'

Lewis felt the same way.

comment in the Bible. Genesis 1:27 says 'So God created man in his own image, in the image of God created he him; male and female created he them.' Some people think this means God created a man and a woman at the same time — which would mean Adam had a wife before Eve was created from Adam's rib, as described later in Genesis.

Lewis didn't agree with that interpretation of the Bible text, but he knew it offered story-telling possibilities. He was aware of the many Lilith stories connected to Adam. In all of them, Lilith is an evil creature, an abomination, disobedient to Adam and to God. Here's a version from Robert Graves and Raphael Patai:

> God then formed Lilith, the first woman, just as He had formed Adam, except that He used filth and sediment instead of pure dust. From Adam's union with this demoness, and with another like her named Naamah, Tubal Cain's sister, sprang Asmodeus and innumerable demons that still plague mankind. Many generations later, Lilith and Naamah came to Solomon's judgement seat, disguised as harlots of Jerusalem.

Poet Dante Gabriel Rossetti, retelling the story of Adam and Eve in his poem 'Eden Bower', put Lilith at the centre. She actually tempts the serpent to tempt Eve! *'Not a drop of her blood was human, / But she was made like a soft sweet woman . . .'* 'Eden Bower' (1869).

Adam and Lilith never found peace together . . . .

In this version, angels remove Lilith from the story to make way for Eve.

Lilith's great offence, many writers have noted, was to demand that Adam treat her as an equal. Some recent retellings of the story show her as a strong, admirable person rather than a demon. What, precisely, was wrong about equality? And was she really made of filth and sediment, or is that just what Adam said after she left him? There are two sides to every story, right?

Lewis didn't see it that way. He held with the severe and traditional view of Lilith. Lewis scholar Peter Schakel explains how Lewis's ideas are connected to Jadis:

> '[Lilith] refused to be subordinate to Adam and to accept her roles as wife and mother. Jadis, in that tradition, opposes life and growth. She thrives in a world of cruelty and death, the kind of world she turned Charn into, but in the Wood between the Worlds, a womb-like area so full of latent life that "you could almost feel the trees growing" (p.29), she loses

George MacDonald (1824–1905), an influential fantasy writer Lewis admired, wrote a novel titled *Lilith* (1895). His version of the character becomes a vampirish monster.

Despite barely being mentioned in the Bible or other common religious texts, the character of Lilith fascinated Lewis. He wrote a poem about her that he put in his novel *The Pilgrim's Regress*, and he referred to her in letters a few times. 'Lilith is still quite beyond me,' he once wrote. To him, she was 'the real ideal somehow spoiled' (*The Collected Letters of C. S. Lewis, Volume 2*, p.119).

her beauty and finds it hard to breathe, "as if the air of that place stifled her". . . Hers is the nature of the seductress, proud, cruel, destructive, oblivious to the need for fair play and harmony between herself and other individuals'.

THE DEVIL MADE ME DO IT

Finally, given Narnia's many connections to the Bible, it's reasonable to wonder if Lewis also meant Jadis to be a stand-in for Satan. There are scholars who reject this connection, but the objections usually come down to quibbles. For instance, it has been said that Jadis can't be a version of Satan, because, as the daughter of Lilith, she is human. That's asking too much accuracy from Lewis. He didn't follow biblical details to the letter. Jadis certainly takes Satan's role in the story. She wants to rule the world; she knows that claiming Edmund will help her; she tempts him with something sweet like Satan tempted Eve with an apple; she's defeated when Aslan gives his life to save Edmund's soul. Though Jadis has several other conscious sources, she's meant to be satanic too.

WHAT IS
DEEP MAGIC?

LWW:
Deep Magic

In Narnia the important magic has nothing to do with wands or broomsticks. The powerful forces Lewis calls 'Deep Magic' and 'Deeper Magic' aren't related to obvious enchantments like the wardrobe that opens into a snowy wood. Those terms refer to ideas at the core of Lewis's philosophy.

DEEP MAGIC

Deep Magic describes an idea known as Natural Law. This is the notion that basic rules about right and wrong are understood by all people, everywhere, because the rules come from a source greater than humankind. 'I hold this conception to be basic to all civilization,' Lewis said (*God in the Dock,* p.318). To Lewis, this universal code is evidence of God, and being from God, it's to be obeyed. Scholar Kathryn Lindskoog says, 'From his first book of prose (*The Pilgrim's Regress,* 1933) to his last

St Thomas Aquinas (1225–74) is often quoted on Natural Law: 'Through it we know what we must do and what we must avoid. God has given this light or law at the Creation.'

article ('We Have No Right To Happiness', 1963), Natural Law was the foundation for much of what he had to say. Natural Law was the first topic of his popular wartime [radio] broadcasts eventually published as *Mere Christianity*.' As Lindskoog puts it, Lewis believed 'there has never been and never will be a radically new value or value system' (*The C. S. Lewis Readers' Encyclopedia*, p.290).

CHEATING THE HANGMAN

In *The Lion, the Witch and the Wardrobe*, Natural Law almosts costs Edmund his life. Desperate for more of the witch's enchanted Turkish Delight, he deserts his brother and sisters and betrays their plans to the witch. As Jadis reminds Aslan, 'You know that every traitor belongs to me as my lawful prey and that for every treachery I have a right to a kill' (*The Lion, the Witch and the Wardrobe*, ch.13). That's Deep Magic, Natural Law.

Traitors belong to Jadis because she's playing the role of Satan. As told in the Bible story of Job, God allowed Satan to test people's souls, and to take those souls if the person failed. This is why Mr Beaver calls Jadis 'the Emperor's hangman' (*The Lion, the Witch and the Wardrobe*, ch.13). He's referring to the 'Emperor-beyond-the-Sea', one of the names

Execution of traitors happens to be the law in our world too. Even some countries that have abolished the death sentence for murder still keep laws that let it be used for treason. In Great Britain capital punishment for treason was still permitted after the abolition of capital punishment for murder in 1965.

of God in Narnia. Edmund has failed the test, so his life and his soul belong to Jadis.

Or so Jadis thinks. Jadis knows a lot, but she makes the mistake of thinking she knows everything. Although her knowledge stretches back to 'the dawn of time' (*The Lion, the Witch and the Wardrobe*, ch.15), that's not far enough. There was a time before the dawn of time, Lewis believed. Only God existed then. Jadis doesn't know all that God knows.

Aslan understands this. He knows that Natural Law was established by the Emperor, God, and that the Emperor is not ruled by it. The Emperor can overrule it with a deeper magic that allows good to triumph over evil, not as a matter of right or wrong, but simply as a matter of the Emperor's will. This is the Narnian version of Lewis's belief in God's grace – a gift of supernatural help to the faithful. As Aslan explains, if a willing and innocent victim agrees to die in the place of the traitor, the Emperor's grace will be granted.

As important as Natural Law was to Lewis, Deeper Magic was more important. In Lewis's view, we are all children of Eve, and all born with sin because Eve ate the apple offered by the serpent in Eden, just as Edmund ate Jadis's Turkish Delight. He believed our only hope

Mere execution was once considered too good for traitors. In Elizabethan England, they were hanged by the neck only until they were almost dead; then they were dragged through the streets by a horse-drawn cart. Finally, while still alive, they were cut into four pieces. (This is the origin of the phrase 'hanged, drawn and quartered'.)

Many American readers are puzzled by Turkish Delight, which isn't nearly as well known in the US as in the UK. The sweet, which is a soft, sweet jelly cube, rolled in powdered sugar, really is from Turkey. There it's known as *lokum* (from the word for 'morsel'), or *rahat lokum* ('morsel of contentment'). It's credited to a Hadji Bekir, a famous confectionery maker from the 1700s, whose family still has a shop in Istanbul.

was for God's grace, which would be given to anyone who has faith in the story that an innocent victim, Christ, died for us.

In naming this rule Deeper Magic, and describing it as a secret that Aslan knew and Jadis didn't, Lewis was following the Bible, which says, 'But we speak the wisdom of God in a mystery, even the hidden wisdom, which God ordained before the world unto our glory; which none of the princes of this world knew: for had they known it, they would not have crucified the Lord of glory' (I Corinthians 2:7–8).

DOES ASLAN FEAR DEATH?

If a reader notices only one biblical allusion in the *Chronicles*, it's that Aslan dies and is resurrected. You don't have to be Christian to spot that. This is surely the most important episode in *The Lion, the Witch and the Wardrobe*. Everything leads up to it. It expresses the central idea of Lewis's belief. Yet even for readers who see it coming, this episode can be surprising. Lewis is unashamedly sentimental in his description of Aslan's death and rebirth. He doesn't want to present mere facts. He doesn't want to make an intellectual argument. The story of the resurrection filled him with emotion, and he wanted readers to have the same experience.

Aslan's Stone Table is carved with the laws of Deep Magic, just as in the Old Testament Moses' Ten Commandments are carved into stone tablets.

ONCE MORE, WITH FEELING

Lewis's close reading of the Bible was the source for both what happens to Aslan and also the feelings he and Lucy and Susan experience.

For many years, US editions said the laws of Deep Magic are carved into the World Ash Tree, which would be Yggdrasil, the tree that in Norse myth holds up the world. The original UK editions say 'fire-stones'. It's not clear who made the change. It upsets some Lewis fans, maybe because in Norse myth the god Odin sacrificed himself on Yggdrasil to gain knowledge, not to save souls.

The night before he's to die, Aslan takes a walk. He thinks he's alone, but Lucy and Susan are following him. He's about to send them away when he reconsiders. 'I should be glad of company tonight,' he says. 'I am sad and lonely' (*The Lion, the Witch and the Wardrobe*, ch.14). When his execution begins, Lucy and Susan watch helplessly as he's tied up, muzzled, shaved, spat on and battered by a jeering crowd.

According to the Book of Matthew, the night before his arrest Christ told a few of his disciples, 'My soul is overwhelmed with sorrow to the point of death' (Matthew 26:38). Then he asked them to walk with him. Later he's said to have suffered humiliations similar to Aslan's: 'Then the governor's soldiers took Jesus into the Praetorium and gathered the whole company of soldiers around him. They stripped him and put a scarlet robe on him, and then twisted together a crown of thorns and set it on his head. They put a staff in his right hand and knelt in front of him and mocked him. "Hail, king of the Jews!" they said. They spit on him, and took the staff and struck him on the head again and again' (Matthew 27:27–31).

Lucy and Susan are like two of Jesus's disciples. In the Narnian version, Lucy and

Susan can barely watch the execution, but they force themselves to witness it. After Aslan's death, they do their best to take care of his battered body. The next day, when 'the rising of the sun had made everything look so different' (*The Lion, the Witch and the Wardrobe*, ch.15), they're overjoyed to discover Aslan is alive again. In the Bible, faithful women disciples 'watch from a distance' as Christ is crucified. Then two of them prepare to tend to his body before discovering he's alive again. It's the rising of the Son, and for the disciples it makes everything look so different.

ONLY HUMAN

As important as the resurrection episode is to the *Chronicles*, something about it has always struck me as odd. For me, Aslan's emotions don't fit with the story. They seem to undermine a basic message of the *Chronicles*.

Lewis gives Aslan the emotions Jesus is said to have felt. But many details of Aslan's experience aren't the same as in the Bible story. Aslan isn't betrayed before his execution. Although Edmund was a traitor to his family, he didn't betray Aslan as Judas betrayed Jesus. Aslan chose execution, rather than having it forced upon him. And the night before the execution, Lucy and Susan are faithful to him.

The Stone Table on which Aslan dies has several sources. A similar sacrificial table appears in H. Rider Haggard's *King Solomon's Mines*. Lewis knew the legends of England's Table-Mên ('Table-Main'), a granite block where Saxon kings were said to have dined – King Arthur too.

This differs from the Bible story, in which the disciples who walk with Jesus fail to stay awake, and leave him alone.

In giving Aslan the emotions Jesus is said to have felt, without giving him the same good reasons for feeling them, Lewis raises an important question: Why is Aslan so sad and lonely, even with Lucy and Susan's companionship and love? Does Aslan fear death?

One of the most important messages Lewis wanted the *Chronicles* to convey – many would argue that it's the single most important point – is that death is not to be feared because what lies beyond is better. Aslan seems to know that. So why all the worrying? Why is he joyful only *after* he is resurrected?

Paul F. Ford, one of the most insightful scholars of biblical allusions in the *Chronicles*, explains that Lewis is portraying Aslan as some people perceive Christ: as human. In this view, Ford says, Christ 'did not, as a man, know the future . . .' He didn't know his resurrection would follow death. He, too, had to trust 'that his Father had a plan even for dying' (*Companion to Narnia*, p.21). Aslan's sadness, it has been pointed out to me, could be just sadness at the existence of evil, not a feeling for himself.

But as Lewis stressed, Aslan isn't exactly

The breaking in two of the Stone Table is an allusion to the Bible: 'When Jesus had cried out again in a loud voice, he gave up his spirit. At that moment the curtain of the temple was torn in two from top to bottom. The earth shook and the rocks split' (Matthew 27: 50–51).

like Christ, and the *Chronicles* aren't the gospels. It's possible to think, from the way Aslan explains Deeper Magic after coming back to life, that he didn't know about his resurrection when he offered to die for Edmund. It's harder to understand why he felt sad and lonely. At worst, he was facing death. And though he may not have known about Deeper Magic, he knew that by his own rules death was nothing to fear. Did he not trust his Father?

Paul F. Ford's interpretation is undoubtedly what Lewis had in mind. It's also reasonable to believe Aslan is merely sad that Narnia has been spoiled. It just doesn't seem that way to me, no matter how many times I read it.

Although the Stone Table brings to mind the mysterious Stonehenge monument, this common interpretation isn't a symbol Lewis intended. However, it may evoke in a reader exactly the feeling Lewis hoped to stir.

A white hart (another word for stag) with a gold collar was the
emblem of King Richard II (1367–1400). Although he adopted it
from the emblem of his mother, a legend grew that a white hart
had suddenly appeared and saved him from an attack by another
stag he had wounded while hunting.

WHY DOES A WHITE STAG LEAD THE WAY?

LWW:
White Stag

When the Pevensies follow a white stag into the forest at the end of *The Lion, the Witch and the Wardrobe*, they begin to suspect a surprise. All of them agree with Queen Lucy when she says 'it will not go out of my mind that if we pass this post and lantern either we shall find strange adventures or else some great change of our fortunes' (*The Lion, the Witch and the Wardrobe*, ch.17). She's right.

FOLLOW THE LEADER

In folk tales, chasing a stag often leads to an imaginary world or a divine place. That's the stag's plan.

A Scottish folk ballad tells how a man known as Thomas the Rhymer was called to Elfland (fairyland) by a stag. According to the tale, he had been there once before as the lover of the Queen of Elfland, before returning home with the gift of poetry and prophecy.

In *The Horse and His Boy* we learn the Narnian stag's name is Chervy. *Chervus* is Latin for deer.

53

The ballad of Thomas the Rhymer is based on a real person. Thomas Learmont, also known as Thomas of Erceldoune (now Earlston), was a poet and soothsayer in the late 1200s. Ellen Kushner's *Thomas the Rhymer* (1990), winner of the World Fantasy Award, and Diana Wynne-Jones's *Fire and Hemlock* (1984) are modern novels based on him.

When the Queen wanted him to return, she sent two deer to him. He followed the deer into the forest and was never seen again.

In the collection of Welsh stories called the *Mabinogion*, a chieftain catches a white stag that the Lord of the Underworld had been hunting. He apologizes and offers to make amends. The Lord of the Underworld suggests they switch places for a year, and adventures follow for them both.

AT WAR WITH THE SERPENT

More than just magical, stags are divine in early myths. In Celtic mythology, the powerful god Cernunnos was depicted as part-stag, a man with antlers. Because stags lose and re-grow their horns, Cernunnos symbolized resurrection and immortality. As in most ancient cultures, the idea of Cernunnos's divine resurrection was connected to the growing season for crops. Each year, according to some myths, he was born in winter, married a goddess in spring (planting) and died at the end of summer (harvest). It's not surprising that when Christianity reached Europe stories of a new resurrected god would mix with older stories and the stag would remain a symbol.

Another interesting myth strengthened the connection. 'Stags are at war with snakes,' wrote the ancient Roman naturalist Pliny the Elder, 'drawing them out of their holes with the breath of their nostrils.' Pliny is known for repeating tall tales, but the description stuck. Because in the Bible the snake is associated with Satan, the stag's 'war' against snakes made it a symbol of Christ. The symbol is usually a white stag, to suggest divine purity.

The *Physiologus*, an early Christian work that connected animals to religious ideas, added to the stag legends:

> Swimming o'er rivers and travelling the
>   earth in like manner they wander,
> Covering distances great, whenever pas-
>   tures they seek.
> Stepping all in a line, they carry their
>   chins very highly,
> Each one bears on his back [the] chin of
>   the Stag in his rear,
> . . . So all changing in turn, and mutual-
>   ly helping each other,
> None ever fails on the road, travelling the
>   whole of the way,
> In such a way as this each bears, for
>   another, the burden,
> This they do moved by love, teaching us,
>   others to help,

People looking for religious references in the Harry Potter novels have pointed out that in times of great danger Harry is saved by a spirit – J. K. Rowling calls it a 'Patronus' – in the form of a stag.

Thus is the law of our Master Christ to us, proven in Nature.

Naturally, the stag came to represent Christ leading souls through the darkness. Lewis hints at this in *The Horse and His Boy* when he says the Narnian stag is 'a beautiful lordly creature'. We know that Lewis is thinking of his own lord, Christ. By the end of *The Lion, the Witch and the Wardrobe*, Lewis felt that the Pevensies, having learned the outlines of Christianity from Aslan, are ready to follow the white stag.

THE MAGICIAN'S NEPHEW:
LEWIS'S THOUGHTS

A second Narnia book did not come easily to Lewis. He wanted to go back in Narnian time, before the arrival of the Pevensies, to when Professor Kirke was young. The trouble was that he couldn't come up with a plot. As a starting point, he looked at loose ends in *The Lion, the Witch and the Wardrobe*. For instance, why was the lamp-post there? But he struggled to get beyond a clever beginning.

You could even say he failed. He didn't actually write the second story. He wrote the fourth and the fifth, then the third, and then the sixth and seventh. Finally he went back and wrote the second. Except he called it the first.

Confused? Imagine his publishers.

Here's what happened. Because *The Lion, the Witch and the Wardrobe* was originally meant to stand alone, Lewis didn't leave him-

The Kilmer family, to whom *The Magician's Nephew* is dedicated, lived in Washington, DC. They were fans of Lewis's work. Lewis's part in the long correspondence between him and some of the eight Kilmer children became part of his *Letters to Children* (1985).

57

self an obvious place to take the story. Compare Narnia to Tolkien's Middle-earth, for example. In *The Lord of the Rings*, Frodo's quest is clear in the first book of the trilogy and reaches its climax in the final volume. It was all one big story to Tolkien. (His publishers turned it into a trilogy because it was the only way to print it.) Philip Pullman's *His Dark Materials* is the same. When Pullman started the first book he already knew some of the decisions his heroine would face in the final volume. Even the Harry Potter novels, which are separate episodes, have a clear progression. Each school year, Harry's nemesis, Lord Voldemort, becomes stronger. J. K. Rowling knew the general outline of the whole series as she was writing the first book. The *Chronicles* didn't work that way at all.

After *The Lion, the Witch and the Wardrobe*, Lewis tried to write something that has become known as 'The Lefay fragment'. The 'fragment' isn't an object in the story. It refers to the unfinished story itself. In it, a Mrs Lefay is godmother to Digory Kirke, who's an orphan with the power to understand the speech of trees and animals. Bits of this story survived – Pattertwig, the squirrel in *Prince Caspian*, was invented here – but the story was abandoned.

Instead Lewis wrote *Prince Caspian*, then *The Voyage of the 'Dawn Treader'*, then *The Horse and His Boy*, then *The Silver Chair*. He then restarted *The Magician's Nephew*, but put it aside again. He wrote all of *The Last Battle*, about the end of Narnia, before finally finishing the book that described Narnia's creation.

The problem may have been that *The Magician's Nephew* is the most personal of the Narnia books. Lewis's mother, like Digory's, suffered a serious illness. Digory's quest to find a cure mirrors Lewis's desire. Unfortunately, Flora Lewis died when Lewis was not quite ten.

That's what's at the heart of *The Magician's Nephew*. On the surface, it's about the creation of Narnia and the first appearance of evil. Underneath, it's the perfect bookend partner for *The Last Battle*. It's the story of Lewis's first battle. Lewis became angry with God when his mother died. Accepting the loss as God's will was a struggle for him. A lesser struggle, but still difficult, was reliving those feelings when writing what was for him the last of the *Chronicles*.

Lewis's suggested reading order, following Narnian history:
1. *The Magician's Nephew*
2. *The Lion, the Witch and the Wardrobe*
3. *The Horse and His Boy*
4. *Prince Caspian*
5. *The Voyage of the 'Dawn Treader'*
6. *The Silver Chair*
7. *The Last Battle*

WHO WERE THE REAL DIGORY KIRKES?

MN:
Digory Kirke

There are two Digory Kirkes in the *Chronicles*. Professor Kirke of *The Lion, the Witch and the Wardrobe* is a stern lecturer. He tells Peter and Susan to use logic to determine if Lucy's story about a world beyond the wardrobe is true. The young Digory Kirke of *The Magician's Nephew* is not as calculating.

The difference between the two Digorys isn't age. It's even simpler. Lewis didn't originally plan for young Digory and Professor Kirke to be the same character in Narnia. They were based on two very different people, and the characters were joined later. The real young Digory was Lewis. The real Professor Kirke was, in an interesting way, Lewis's opposite.

Because of her affection for the *Chronicles*, J. K. Rowling played with the letters in Digory's name to create the name 'Cedric Diggory' for a heroic classmate of Harry Potter.

THE GREAT KNOCK

Although his own life inspired the premise of *The Lion, the Witch and the Wardrobe* —

Professor Kirke taking in children during the Second World War – Lewis didn't start by making the Professor a self-portrait. Kirke was always based on his mentor, William T. Kirkpatrick (1848–1921).

By the time Lewis was a boy, Kirkpatrick was already retired as headmaster of Lurgan College in Northern Ireland. It was Lewis's father who had originally been one of Kirkpatrick's students. Later his father became Kirkpatrick's lawyer, and Kirkpatrick became a family friend. When Lewis ran into difficulty at boarding school, Kirkpatrick agreed to take him in and tutor him personally.

Kirkpatrick to Lewis's father: 'You may make a writer or a scholar out of him, but you'll not make anything else' (*Surprised by Joy*, p.183).

Kirkpatrick, known to Lewis and his family as Kirk or 'the Great Knock' or just 'Knock', was an intimidating figure who looked and acted much like Professor Kirke of the *Chronicles*. There was no such thing as casual conversation with him. Moments after arriving in Surrey to take up residence with Kirkpatrick, Lewis received his first lesson in logic. Lewis made a friendly comment about the scenery; Kirkpatrick asked him to explain the logic behind it. 'Answer after answer was torn to shreds,' Lewis remembered. 'If ever a man came near to being a purely logical entity, that man was Kirk' (*Surprised by Joy*, pp.129–30).

Lewis grew to love Kirkpatrick's odd manner. He also realized quickly that the education he was receiving, mostly in languages and literature, was exactly what he needed. Kirkpatrick, he said 'taught me to think' (*Miracles*, p.69).

What was left out of the tutoring was just as important. Unlike nearly any formal school Lewis might have attended, Kirkpatrick did not press religion on Lewis. Kirkpatrick was interested in what he could see and explain. Faith in the unseen made no sense to him.

This was a relief to Lewis. At the time he studied with Kirkpatrick, he was an atheist himself, in a peculiar way. Peculiar because he thought of himself as one, but probably wasn't. He was in the middle of religious and psychological battles that wouldn't be settled for good until decades later.

Lewis also turned Kirkpatrick into the firmly logical character MacPhee in two of his science fiction novels, *That Hideous Strength* (1945) and *The Dark Tower* (1977).

THE GREAT ARGUMENT

Throughout *The Magician's Nephew*, Digory is pushed along by his desire to find a cure for his sick mother. He takes risks for her, he makes mistakes for her, and, ultimately, what he learns from Aslan has everything to do with her. He finds a way to accept the possibility that she might die.

All those feelings came from Lewis's own

experience of his mother's death. But just as his story was different from Digory's in the external facts – Digory's mother lives – the internal struggle had a different ending. Digory has faith in Aslan, and stays faithful to him. Lewis didn't. He resented the loss of his mother too much, and grew angry with the God who seemed to ignore his prayers.

Although Lewis later explained his loss of faith with details that might make it seem like a slow process based on rational thought, it's fairly obvious that his mother's death not only started the process but made the rest of it inevitable. Lewis became an atheist out of anger, which made him a peculiar kind of atheist. It's impossible to be angry with God and yet at the same time deny his existence. That's like running into your bedroom after an argument with your parents and thinking that slamming the door makes them disappear.

Looking back as an adult, Lewis said that from Kirkpatrick he received 'fresh ammunition for a position already chosen'. Kirkpatrick's ammunition was the sort found in an influential study of ancient cultures called *The Golden Bough* (1890). The author, Sir James George Frazer (1854–1941), showed example after example of parallels between

Kirkpatrick's school, Lurgan College, was founded in 1873 by a grant that prohibited clergyman teachers or religious instruction. This was exceptional. Defying expectations, Kirkpatrick did require that students attend religious classes during non-school hours.

pre-Christian religions and Christianity. To Kirkpatrick, this was a sign that Chrisitianity was nothing special.

Years later, when his faith returned, Lewis turned all that evidence around. He decided all those pre-Christian traditions were just foreshadowing of a true religion to come. He said all a person had to do to see that ideas about good and evil are universal – and therefore from God, in his view – was to read the *Encyclopedia of Religion and Ethics*.

It's the adult Lewis who forces Digory to accept that Aslan's law – don't steal the apple – is more important than using the apple to heal his mother. 'He gave up all hopes of saving his Mother's life; but at the same time he knew that the Lion knew what would have happened, and that there might be things more terrible even than losing someone you love by death' (*The Magician's Nephew*, ch.14).

Without a doubt, Lewis's struggle to write *The Magician's Nephew* was a struggle to face those childhood emotions. Even after years of faith his feelings were still sore.

The Great Knock might not have understood. But as an adult, Lewis was sentimental about his remote, intimidating mentor. 'My reverence to this day [is] undiminished,' he said (*Surprised by Joy*, p.148).

The death of his mother did not make Lewis a literal orphan like young Digory. But the emotional truth was the same. Within two weeks of his mother's death he was sent from his home in Ireland to a boarding school in England that he later described as a 'concentration camp'.

Reading the *Chronicles*, it's easy to see that part of Lewis always remained nine years old. The blow of his mother's death probably made that inevitable. It may explain his devotion to the past – as novelist and former Lewis student Penelope Fitzgerald put it, Lewis 'made a "thing" of disliking the twentieth century' (*The Afterlife*, p.250). It may also explain why he had to finish the *Chronicles* where they began, and why that was so hard. Another great teacher, the American educator Mark Hopkins, once said, 'Among the last things that a man comes to know thoroughly is himself.'

Kirkpatrick shared the dismal opinion about modern education that was voiced by Professor Kirke.

WHO SAW THE FIRST INKLING OF NARNIA?

Other writers might have invented a single rule for moving characters into Narnia and out of it. Lewis invented new tricks whenever he felt like it: a wardrobe, a painting, the call of a horn, magic rings. This casual attitude towards the rules of Narnia is one reason Lewis's friend J. R. R. Tolkien didn't love the *Chronicles*.

Tolkien might have laughed by the time he read *The Magician's Nephew*. The magical green rings and gold rings that transport Digory Kirke and Polly Plummer to Narnia and back are a sly tribute to Tolkien's *The Hobbit* and *The Lord of the Rings*. That tribute isn't the only one. Lewis and Tolkien had a friendship and an informal working relationship that was very important to both men, personally and professionally. It altered their careers. It changed Lewis's life.

Biographer Humphrey Carpenter says the blustery voice of Treebeard, the tree guardian in *The Lord of the Rings*, was meant to mimic Lewis's booming voice.

Lewis and Tolkien were brought together by a love of adventure. Armchair adventure, that is. They met in Oxford, where Tolkien was a professor of Anglo-Saxon (Old English). Both, they discovered, adored Norse myths – Old Icelandic sagas about gods and heroes. Tolkien asked Lewis to be part of a group he was forming that would read these sagas in the original Old Icelandic.

Both men were clubby. Lewis loved rowdy conversations about literature fuelled with beer. Tolkien had been forming groups to talk about literature since he was a schoolboy. Both agreed: no girls allowed.

Tolkien's club was called the Kolbítars ('Coalbiters'), an old Icelandic term for tale-swappers who sat so close to the fire that they could bite the coals. Once a week the friends would gather by a fireplace in their slippers, beer at the ready, and read aloud. For Lewis, reading 'the mere names of god and giant' in Icelandic was enough to give him a thrill.

Another club, which has since become famous in literary circles, grew out of this friendship in the mid-1930s. It was called the Inklings, which Tolkien said was a pun referring to 'people with vague or half-formed intimations and ideas plus those who dabble

Lewis considered long, loud, drunken evenings with students and other scholars – he called them 'English binges' – to be a kind of 'folk-art'. They were a common part of his life at Oxford.

in ink'. One evening each week (and often another morning too) they met at a pub to drink, talk and read to each other whatever they were writing.

Even within the club, Lewis and Tolkien had special influence on each other's work. They didn't always see eye to eye, but that didn't matter to either of them. Lewis once observed, 'The man who agrees with us that some question, little regarded by others, is of great importance can be our Friend. He need not agree with us about the answer' (*The Four Loves*, p.66).

THE SINCEREST FORM OF FRIENDSHIP

Lewis was a great encourager of Tolkien, who was obsessed with creating a whole set of myths about ancient Britain, despite the lack of interest from his publishers. Then, having encouraged Tolkien, Lewis drew on Tolkien's creations just as he drew on classical myths and Icelandic sagas. Long before *The Lord of the Rings* was published, Lewis published books that alluded to it. As far as Lewis was concerned, Tolkien's myths were as real as the others. He might have held that opinion even if he wasn't Tolkien's friend; but of course he knew all about Tolkien's painstaking scholarship. Naturally, given their many discussions

'Inklings' had been coined in about 1931 by student Edward Tangye Lean for a club that broke up a few years before Tolkien and Lewis adopted the name.

The Inklings met
until the late
1940s. Over
time, there were
about a dozen
Inklings.
Members
included:
Lewis's brother
Warren; Charles
Williams, an
author and an
editor at Oxford
University Press;
Owen Barfield,
Lewis's good
friend and
intellectual
sparring partner;
Lord David
Cecil, an Oxford
lecturer and
author;
Nevill Coghill,
professor of
English and also
a theatre
director.

during the course of Tolkien's work, Lewis's allusions get right to the heart of Tolkien's world.

HERE COME THE FLOODS

From childhood, Tolkien was haunted by a dream of a huge, dangerous wave. He came to believe it was an ancestral memory, and that it was connected to the myth of the lost island Atlantis, where a great civilization is said to have been wiped out in an instant. His efforts to understand the dream led him to write myths about Atlantis, which in his version was called Númenor.

One of its first appearances followed a challenge from Lewis during an Inklings meeting. Somehow a discussion led Lewis to say, 'One of us should write a tale of time travel and the other should do space travel.' (The Inklings drank a lot during their meetings.) They flipped a coin and Tolkien drew the time travel. Woven into his story, 'The Lost Road', was the tale of noble men on an island called Númenor. An evil wizard Sauron – the great enemy of *The Lord of the Rings* – corrupts the men, which prompts the God of Middle-earth to sink Númenor under a great wave.

Lewis heard about Númenor when Tolkien

read the story to his fellow Inklings. He liked Tolkien's version of the Atlantean myth so much that when he turned his space-travel story into a novel he included references to 'Numinor' and 'the last vestiges of Atlantean magic'. (The spelling is different because Lewis had only heard the story read aloud.) In the book's introduction, he gave readers a teaser about Tolkien's work. 'Those who would like to learn further about Numinor and the True West must (alas!) await the publication of much that exists only in the MSS. [manuscripts] of my friend, Professor J. R. R. Tolkien' (*That Hideous Strength*, p.7).

PETRIFYING FORESTS

Tolkien hated the way humankind treats nature. His anger is apparent throughout *The Lord of the Rings*. He got his revenge by bringing a forest to life, and turning it into an army that comes to the rescue of the heroes:

There is a great power in them, and they seem able to wrap themselves in shadow: it is difficult to see them moving. But they do. They can move very quickly, if they are angry. You stand still looking at the weather, maybe, or listening to the

Many cultures – Mesopotamian, Greek, Scandinavian, Indian, Chinese, even Australian aborigines – have a story about an ancient great flood that almost wiped out mankind. The story of Noah's Ark is just one of them.

rustling of the wind, and then suddenly you find that you are in the middle of a wood with great groping trees all around you.

Lewis admired Tolkien's view on nature, and echoed Tolkien's passion by describing the sudden appearance of a powerful forest in much the same way in *Prince Caspian*:

> (I)magine that (a) wood, instead of being fixed to one place, was rushing at you . . . their long arms waved like branches . . .
> (*Prince Caspian*, ch.14)

The forest has the same effect on the evil armies in both tales. Tolkien expresses his anger by having the trees attack the Orcs in *The Lord of the Rings*:

> The Orcs reeled and screamed and cast aside both sword and spear. Like a black smoke driven by a mounting wind they fled. Wailing they passed under the waiting shadow of the trees; and from that shadow none ever came again.

In *Prince Caspian*, Lewis mirrors the action as the trees take on the Telemarines:

Tolkien got the idea of a walking forest from watching Shakespeare's *Macbeth*. In the play, there's a prophecy about a forest that marches and later, an army camouflages itself with twigs and branches. Tolkien felt cheated by the clever way the prophecy came true. He wanted to see an army of real trees. So he created one in his book.

72

Tough looking warriors . . . flung down their weapons, shrieking, 'The Wood! The Wood! . . .'

But soon neither their cries nor the sound of weapons could be heard (above) the ocean-like roar of the Awakened Trees . . . (*Prince Caspian*, ch.14)

WEDDED RINGS

In *The Lord of the Rings*, Tolkien added a twist to the Icelandic sagas he and Lewis shared. Tolkien's version was to find its way into Lewis's *The Magician's Nephew* and *The Voyage of the 'Dawn Treader'*.

There's a famous story in the sagas about a magic ring that offers great wealth but which is cursed to cause tragedy for any mortal who wears it. Tolkien's first novel of Middle-earth, *The Hobbit*, made that ring a small part of the plot. Then, in the course of writing *The Lord of the Rings*, the importance of the ring grew, and its meaning changed. Tolkien added a Christian interpretation: the rings (there were several in Tolkien's novel) were made through the trickery of Sauron, whose 'lust and pride . . . knew no bounds' and who wants to take God's role in Middle-earth. His arrogance affects all the wearers of the rings. They, too, deceive themselves into thinking they deserve

In at least one important way, Lewis's work was the opposite of Tolkien's. Lewis's villains are, for the most part, evil humans from different lands or cultures than the heroes. Tolkien felt strongly that humans were more weak than evil. In his Middle-earth, the humans and all the other creatures consciously set aside their differences to defeat evil's true satanic source.

Readers had to wait a long time for Tolkien's version of the Atlantis myth. Tolkien tried to turn the time-travel story into a novel, but abandoned it after four chapters. Númenor's story, important as it is to the background of Middle-earth, also was left out of *The Lord of the Rings*. It was finally published in *The Silmarillion*, more than thirty years after Lewis's version had appeared.

glory, and into believing themselves strong enough to control the magic of the ring. Naturally, most of them are led to ruin.

The story of the rings in *The Magician's Nephew* reveals a similar arrogance: a foolhardy pursuit of 'knowledge' that Lewis, like Tolkien, believed was God's alone. Lewis's rings are made from Atlantean dust with 'hidden wisdom'. Another sinful ring causes Eustace trouble in *The Voyage of the 'Dawn Treader'*. (See p.137.)

CONVERSATION TO CONVERSION

If all we did was look at their books, we could be cynical about the friendship between Lewis and Tolkien. Lewis borrowed a lot from his friend. He sometimes wrote passages that were close to what he'd heard Tolkien read. What he took was at the core of Tolkien's work. And he published books that drew on Tolkien's works before Tolkien had finished writing. But we'd be wrong to look at their friendship as competitive. Tolkien and Lewis didn't. Tolkien believed he owed more of a professional debt to Lewis than Lewis owed him. Lewis was a great encourager of Tolkien. Borrowing from Tolkien's myths was a way of letting Tolkien know he believed the myths were as valid as the classics. Tolkien understood the compliment. He needed that encouragement during the dozen years it took him to write *The Lord of the Rings*. 'Only from him did I ever get the idea that my "stuff" could be more than a private hobby,' Tolkien wrote. 'But for his interest and unceasing eagerness for more I should never have brought The L. of the R. to a conclusion . . .'

The real debt Lewis owed Tolkien was personal. The myths he took from Middle-earth weren't as important to him as another myth Tolkien gave him one night. On 19 September 1931, Tolkien, along with another friend, Hugo Dyson, brought Lewis back to Christianity. As they had dinner and went for a walk they discussed mythology and religious faith. Although by 1929 Lewis had moved from an avowed atheism to accepting the idea of the divine, he continued to think of Christianity as just another myth. He didn't see how Christ was more than a good example to people. The dynamic of death and salvation left him cold. Christianity, to him, was just another story like others before it. Tolkien disagreed. He argued that since man comes from God, there is always an essential truth in pagan myths. Since Lewis was moved by pagan myths of sacrifice to a feeling 'profound and suggestive of meanings beyond my grasp,' he should feel the

Lewis met Henry 'Hugo' Dyson (1896–1975), who taught at Reading University, in 1930, when Dyson was in Oxford as a visiting lecturer. They hit it off immediately. In 1945 Dyson took a permanent post at Oxford.

same about the story of Christ (*The Collected Letters of C. S. Lewis, Volume 1*, p.977). Tolkien said Lewis should feel even more profoundly about Christ.

There's no record of exactly what evidence Tolkien presented to back up the last part of that argument. As Lewis himself explained many years later, you have to believe in miracles to accept it. But people who want to believe in miracles have no trouble finding evidence for them, and long before the conversation took place Lewis wanted to believe. From conversation to 'conversion', as Lewis called it, didn't take long. Two weeks later, Lewis told a friend he had once again fully embraced Christianity: 'My long night talk with Dyson and Tolkien had a good deal to do with it.'

Lewis: 'It is inaccurate to define a miracle as something that breaks the laws of Nature' (*Miracles*, p.59).

WHO LET EVIL INTO NARNIA?

MN:
Mrs Lefay

Lewis loved the tales of King Arthur, and he often drew on them for his books. He wrote a long poem about one of Arthur's knights, Lancelot; in one of his science-fiction novels, he imagined that part of Arthur's kingdom still existed; and the first draft of *The Magician's Nephew* began with Digory being visited by a magician from Arthur's world who was far more powerful than Digory's Uncle Andrew.

That early draft, which Lewis abandoned, is the 'Lefay fragment', named after a character who's mentioned only briefly in the final version of the book. In the early draft she's Digory's good godmother. By the final version she was Uncle Andrew's godmother, and not necessarily good. She has done 'very unwise' things, so some unknown authority 'shut her up' (*The Magician's Nephew*, ch.2).

That's closer to some of the legends on

In the Lefay fragment, Mrs Lefay, as Digory's godmother, appears to be the opposite of her role in *The Magician's Nephew*. Her scene is brief and unfinished, but she's pushing Digory to do right – or at least admonishing him for doing wrong.

which she was based. Mrs Lefay is Morgan Le Fay from the tales of Arthur. Though Morgan Le Fay could sometimes be helpful, she was also treacherous. It's no surprise that Mrs Lefay is the source of the magic that eventually brought evil into Narnia.

The name 'Fay' is a sign of her magical power. It means 'fairy'. Morgan Le Fay of the Arthur legends is a great sorceress who learned some of her magic from Merlin. She's the Queen of Avalon, the enchanted land where heroes are rewarded before death. Some legends say she's Arthur's half-sister, and she's often his rival. In some legends she tries to steal Arthur's sword, Excalibur. She even tries to kill him. But she also uses her special gifts of healing to help Arthur when he is mortally wounded.

An interesting detail: some legends about Morgan Le Fay are borrowed from ancient Greek stories about the great sorceress Medea. Both women cast a spell on a cloak so that it will burst into flames and kill whoever wears it.

Lewis borrowed a different Greek myth for his Mrs Lefay of the *Chronicles*. The box she gives to Uncle Andrew, which she makes him promise to destroy in a special ritual, is Lewis's version of the Greek story about Pandora's box. In the original myth, Pandora is the first

Some scholars believe Morgan Le Fay derives from stories about Mórrígan, an Irish war goddess. Mórrígan was said to take the shape of a crow or raven and fly over battlefields. She might then pick who would die, or claim the heads of the dead as trophies.

woman, created by the gods to make things difficult for mankind, who existed in a world without fear or disease or violence. Besides beauty, the gods give Pandora curiosity. Then they put into a box many harmful things, like sorrow, hate, jealousy, cruelty, pain, old age and death. They forbid her from opening it, but know she will. When she does, the horrible things which fly out begin to plague

In the earliest Arthur stories, Morgan is usually on the side of good. She was made more of a villain with each new telling. In the twentieth century, when female authors such as Marion Zimmer Bradley began to retell the stories from Morgan's perspective, Morgan became a heroine again.

Morgan Le Fay tried to kill Arthur by sending him a cloak that would burst into flames. Arthur asked a court maiden to try it on first.

mankind. Fortunately, the last thing in the box is hope. Pandora lets it fly out too. People might suffer all sorts of dreadful things because of her, but they also have hope to keep them from despair.

Lewis added that story to the Le Fay tradition because it's the classical version of the story of Eve. When Eve was tempted with the apple that represented knowledge, she was acting as Pandora did.

Uncle Andrew gives in to the temptation of the box. Digory gives in to the temptation to strike the golden bell with the hammer, bringing evil into Narnia by awakening Jadis, but resists the temptation to create further mayhem by taking the magic apple to his mother.

Pandora's name means 'all gifts' – a sly joke by the gods.

WHY DOES ASLAN'S BREATH MAKE ANIMALS SPEAK?

MN:
Creation

Lions are universal symbols of great strength, but Aslan performs some of his greatest feats delicately. In *The Lion, the Witch and the Wardrobe*, he brings Jadis's stone prisoners back to life simply by breathing on them (*The Lion, the Witch and the Wardrobe*, ch.16). His breath gives strength during difficult times, such as when Lucy's afraid on the Dark Island in *The Voyage of the 'Dawn Treader'* (*The Voyage of the 'Dawn Treader'*, ch.12). In *Prince Caspian*, he reassures Susan that he has returned to life with 'his warm breath' (*Prince Caspian*, ch.10). In the same book, his breath makes Edmund appear to be 'a very dangerous knight' to his Telamarine enemies (*Prince Caspian*, ch.13). The list goes on. In *The Companion to Narnia*, Paul F. Ford identifies about a dozen examples of Aslan performing

J. R. R. Tolkien wrote an origin myth for Middle-earth that may have inspired Lewis to have Aslan sing the creation of Narnia. In Tolkien's myth, it's angels who sing to create the universe.

wonders with his breath. Perhaps the greatest of these incidents occurs in *The Magician's Nephew*. With a 'long, warm breath', Aslan brings all of Narnia to life (*The Magician's Nephew*, ch.9).

For Lewis, Aslan's breath represented something very specific at the centre of his beliefs. It's the Holy Spirit, one of the three forms of God. (Lewis believed in a Trinity, meaning he believed God existed in three forms, equally and at the same time: God, the Father; Jesus, the Son; and the Holy Spirit.) Lewis expert Walter Hooper explains that 'Spirit' and 'Ghost' are translations of early Hebrew and Greek Bible references to a 'breath' or 'air' (*rauch* in Hebrew; *pneuma* in Greek).

Both Hooper and scholar Paul F. Ford, who come to the *Chronicles* as devout Christians, are especially moved by a particular moment in *The Horse and His Boy*. Shasta asks 'Who are you?' in the darkness, because he can't tell who is walking beside him. A voice answers 'Myself' three times. 'The leaves rustled' at the third answer, as if it were spoken by a wind (*The Horse and His Boy*, ch.11).

For Lewis too, it meant a lot to feel what couldn't be seen. This goes back to a central scene in the Bible, when Jesus meets his disci-

Some Christians refer to the Holy Spirit as the Holy Ghost. That was the common translation until a bit more than a century ago. It's what appears in the King James Version of the Bible (1611). But as 'ghost' came to be more associated with a Hallowe'en creature than a living person's soul, 'Holy Spirit' began to appear in new translations.

ples after the Resurrection, Jesus 'breathed on them, and says unto them, Receive the Holy Spirit' (John 20:22).

And what about the animals? As both Hooper and Ford also note, the moment when Aslan's breath gives the power of speech to the animals of Narnia – when his 'long, warm breath' was followed by a 'swift flash of fire . . . either from the sky or from the Lion itself' (*The Magician's Nephew*, ch.9) – is another reference to the Holy Ghost:

In *The Lion, the Witch and the Wardrobe,* Father Christmas gives the Pevensies gifts of armour and weapons that are associated with the Holy Spirit in a Bible passage (Ephesians 6:10–18). This leads some people to take Father Christmas as an actual symbol of the Holy Spirit – an interpretation that may be stretching things too far.

And when the day of Pentecost [a special feast day] was fully come, they [Christ's disciples] were all with one accord in one place.

And suddenly there came a sound from heaven as of a rushing mighty wind, and it filled all the house where they were sitting.

And there appeared unto them cloven tongues like as of fire, and it sat upon each of them.

And they were all filled with the Holy Ghost, and began to speak with other tongues, as the Spirit gave them utterance (Acts 2, 1–4).

WHY DID CHARN GO FROM BAD TO WORSE?

Digory and Polly get a spooky feeling as they walk through the Hall of Images in Charn, where hundreds of people sit spellbound, 'like the most wonderful waxworks' (*The Magician's Nephew*, ch.4). The expressions of the first people they pass look 'kind and wise', but as Polly and Digory move down the rows the expressions become 'solemn', then 'cruel', then 'despairing' and 'dreadful'. This awful tour ends when they come upon Jadis, spellbound as the others, waiting for someone to strike the bell with the hammer.

Although Jadis is the star of the show, even before the spell is broken, those hundreds of people are more than just an eerie backdrop. They may be an allusion to one of the great classical myths.

Clare Hulton, a children's literature expert, notes that the people in the room follow the descriptions of the Five Ages of Man, described by the Greek writer Hesiod in the seventh century BC. In Hesiod's dark view, humankind had degenerated from era to era. These are the ages of humankind he described in his *Works and Days*:

The Golden Age. This first age was perfection. 'A golden race' of humankind was made by Cronos (the Roman god Saturn). These humans lived like gods. There was no need to work, because the earth provided everything they needed. They lived without sorrow. They didn't age. Every day was full of joy. Death was as peaceful as falling asleep.

The Silver Age. The humans of the second age, made by Cronos's son, Zeus (Jupiter), were 'of silver and less noble by far'. Childhood lasted a hundred years, and children were left uneducated. Life was short and sad after that because these people were foolish. They sinned against each other and the gods. Zeus created the seasons to make them suffer the extremes of summer and winter, and forced them to work. These people were strong but mentally weak, powerful but disrespectful. Zeus sent them to the underworld.

Lewis refers to Narnia's early days of glory as 'the Golden Age'. In *Prince Caspian* and *The Voyage of the 'Dawn Treader'*, set many years after *The Lion, the Witch and the Wardrobe* in Narnian time, Caspian is desperate to restore the Golden Age.

The Bronze Age. Zeus created another race of humans, from ash-trees. It was not equal even to the Silver Age. The people were 'terrible and strong'. They were followers of Ares (Mars), god of war. They were rock-hard and cruel. 'Their armour was of bronze, and their houses of bronze, and of bronze were their implements.' But they too disappeared. 'Terrible though they were, Death seized them, and they left the bright light of the sun.'

The Heroic Age. This fourth age of humankind also fell short of the Golden Age, but was superior to the Silver and Bronze Ages. This was the age of demi-gods and heroes. Zeus created people who were 'nobler and more righteous'. They fought epic battles like the one at Troy. Zeus rewarded them by sending their dead to a land for heroes.

The Iron Age. The fifth age was Hesiod's and ours. Hesiod says it's the worst age of all. It's filled with deceit, and crime, and despair. People are selfish and violent.

The father will not agree with his children, nor the children with their father, nor comrade with comrade; nor will brother be dear to brother as before. Men will dishonour their parents, and will carp at them, chiding them with bitter words,

In *King Solomon's Mines,* an H. Rider Haggard novel Lewis reread often, the hero finds a cave in which dead kings have been placed around a table. The corpses have been petrified by the dripping from rocks above, which have formed stalagmites over them. At the head of the table sits a sculpture of Death.

hard-hearted they, not knowing the fear of the gods. Might shall be right, and one man will sack another's city. There will be no favour for the man who keeps his oath or for the just or for the good; but rather men will praise the evil-doer and his violent dealing. Reverence will cease to be. The wicked will hurt the worthy man, speaking false words against him, and will swear an oath upon them. Envy, foul-mouthed, delighting in evil, with scowling face, will go along with wretched men one and all.

In France, Voltaire was the great advocate of the Age of Reason. In Britain, Jonathan Swift and Alexander Pope thumbed their noses at authority.

In Lewis's time, many scholars thought pessimists like Hesiod had it backwards. The trend was to show humankind progressing. This was the central idea of what in the eighteenth century was called a new age, the Age of Reason. Also known as the Enlightenment, this was an intellectual movement based on the notion that humankind could advance towards perfection with earthly logic. Respect for established authority, such as kings or churches, was to be rejected. Religion, for example, might be replaced with a moral code based on natural law, not on a belief in supernatural miracles like the resurrection of God's son. (In Narnian terms, there would be Deep Magic but not Deeper Magic.) The effects of the Enlightenment reached beyond scholars. The revolutions in America and France were due in part to its ideals and to people like Ben Franklin and Thomas Jefferson who were considered part of it.

Lewis wasn't so sure humankind was changing for the better, or that it could. He didn't believe that religion should take its authority only from the will of the people. (For that matter, he didn't think government should take its authority only from the will of the people.) The Age of Reason, as far as Lewis was concerned, made the grave mistake of putting humankind before God.

Like Hesiod, Lewis believed history ran in the opposite direction: God created humankind, which was perfect upon creation but then fell.

'"Dare to use your own understanding!" is the motto of the Enlightenment'. – Immanuel Kant (1724–1804), German philosopher.

WHAT'S THE DEPLORABLE WORD?

MN: Deplorable Word

'In the Beginning was the Word', says the Gospel of St John. In the End, too, according to Jadis.

Just what was the Deplorable Word that Jadis spoke to destroy the land of Charn? Does it relate to a passage in the Bible? Is it a witch's spell? Is it a symbol for something? Lewis never explained it, so there's a lot of conjecture among fans. The answer isn't as obvious as some people believe. It's something that began as an idea, but then became real.

A LITTLE LEARNING IS A DANGEROUS THING

The ancient kings who ruled Charn knew the word existed, but swore 'never even to seek after the knowledge' of it (*The Magician's Nephew*, ch.5). Jadis sought after it and learned it, and when all other efforts to defeat her sister in battle failed, she used it. Every living thing but Jadis was destroyed.

One theory is that the Deplorable Word refers to the Arthurian story of the Dolorous (painful or sorrowful) Stroke: a man attacks a king with the lance that was used to stab Christ during the Crucifixion, and the castle walls suddenly collapse. (See also p.100.)

91

When *The Magician's Nephew* was published in 1955, many readers assumed Lewis was talking about the atomic bomb, invented a decade before. Some scholars agreed the Deplorable Word was a symbol for the bomb.

They were only partly right. Lewis, like many people, was disgusted that the atomic bomb had been invented. He felt humankind was pursuing knowledge too far. But he also minimized it. In a poem he wrote about it he said it was typically human, a 'puny gadget', nothing when compared to the greater, timeless forces of evil in the universe (*The Essential C. S. Lewis*, p.418).

The sudden destruction of Charn isn't meant to symbolize the destruction of Hiroshima and Nagasaki or anything new to the atomic age. Stories like Charn's have been told forever. The story of Atlantis, which fascinated Lewis and his friend Tolkien, was already a legend when Plato recorded it 2,400 years ago. (The story was supposedly 7,000 years old at the time.) As children's literature expert Clare Hulton points out, there's a similar story in the Bible with striking similarities to the story of Charn.

The prophet Nahum, who lived some time around 750–700 BC in Galilee, warned of the impending destruction of the ancient city of

Many readers of *The Lord of the Rings*, published at nearly the same time as the *Chronicles*, are certain the evil and all-powerful One Ring is another symbol of the atomic bomb. Absolutely not, according to Tolkien. It might be possible to apply the lessons from the story to real life, but his Ring was in a draft of the book written long before the bomb was invented.

Nineveh, the capital of the Assyrian Empire. Jadis's description of Charn echoes the descriptions of Nineveh, 'an exceedingly great city' that had become 'all full of lies and robbery'. Just as Charn was 'blotted out' by Jadis, Nineveh was 'empty, and void, and waste'.

In fact, more than a decade before the bomb was created, in 1933, Lewis published a book that included a very similar image of destruction. In his first novel, *The Pilgrim's Regress*, the evil temptress Lilith – who in the *Chronicles* is Jadis's mother – tempts a pilgrim, who is thirsty, with a deadly drink. The pilgrim hesitates, thinking about Lilith's power:

> – Her spells, which all around
> So change the land, we think it
> A great waste where a sound
> Of wind like tales twice told
> Blusters, and cloud is rolled
> Always above yet no rain falls to the
> ground. (*The Pilgrim's Regress*, p.190)

THAT'S MY NAME, DON'T WEAR IT OUT

Lewis's feeling about the atomic bomb may not directly explain the Deplorable Word, but may suggest another way of thinking about it. Lewis was offended when humankind grasped for knowledge that he believed was God's

Paul F. Ford notes the similarity of 'Charn' to the word 'charnel', an old term for burial grounds.

There's even more to it. The medieval texts Lewis studied used 'charnel' to describe the area outside Jerusalem's walls where Christ was crucifed.

(That place was named 'Golgotha' in Hebrew, from the word for skull. Romans called it 'Calvary', from the word for skull in Latin.)

Prometheus is a Titan, one of the elder generation of gods that Zeus and the other Olympians overthrew. To punish him for stealing fire to give to humans, Zeus had him chained to a rock, where an eagle pecked out and ate his liver. Each day the liver grew back; each day the eagle returned. After thirty years on the rock, Hercules freed him. So Zeus created Pandora, with her box of evil, to punish humans directly.

alone. That feeling is actually connected to an ancient taboo. Whether it's the story of Eve and the apple, or the Greek myth of Prometheus stealing fire from the gods for humans, there's a timeless belief that humankind will be punished for attempting to take the power of gods for itself.

In many religions, that taboo is a prohibition against speaking the name of certain gods. 'Gods must keep their true name secret,' wrote anthropologist Sir James George Frazer in *The Golden Bough*, 'lest other gods or even men should learn the mystic sounds and thus be able to conjure with them.' Frazer notes that this taboo is as old as pre-history and as contemporary as modern royal families, whose members are rarely called by name. There's even a connection to an ancient Babylonian and Hebrew myth about Lilith. 'Because Adam tried to compel her obedience by force, Lilith, in a rage, uttered the magic name of God, rose into the air and left him.'

It's Jadis who calls the word 'deplorable'. What would be more deplorable to her than the name of God?

THE HORSE AND HIS BOY:
LEWIS'S THOUGHTS

There are serious things to say about *The Horse and His Boy*, but let's not forget Lewis was also writing for what he called the '"pony-book" public' (*C. S. Lewis: A Companion and Guide*, p.405). The story is three or four popular adventures rolled into one. There's the hidden prince with a royal brother, calling to mind stories as old as the tale of Moses and Pharaoh, or as recent – in Lewis's time – as Mark Twain's *The Prince and the Pauper* (1881), Frances Hodgson Burnett's *Little Lord Fauntleroy* (1886) and Anthony Hope's *The Prisoner of Zenda* (1926). There's *A Thousand and One Arabian Nights*, with the Middle-eastern villains who appear all too often in European stories. And there are the horses.

The 'pony-book' genre is never completely out of style, and it was enjoying a lot of favour when Lewis was thinking up ideas for new

Lewis dedicated *The Horse and His Boy* to David and Douglas Gresham, the sons of his lover, Joy Davidman. (He and Davidman were married after her divorce from her first husband.)

Narnia books. Anna Sewell's *Black Beauty* may have been from another century – it was first published in 1877 – but Enid Bagnold's *National Velvet* (1935) had become a hit film about the time Lewis started the *Chronicles*. Marguerite Henry's *Misty of Chincoteague* (1947) had been instantly (and accurately) hailed as a likely classic. By design, *The Horse and His Boy* is like countless adventures that publishers' advertising departments dare to call 'galloping'.

The elements of the story are simple: two runaways, two talking horses, a desperate escape from an evil land to the glorious Narnia, where one of the runways will be embraced by his lost father and will rule. Add to that a glamorous, veiled girl and a fierce battle. There's nothing left but to leave the audience laughing – which Lewis does.

So it's surprising that *The Horse and His Boy* is one of the most controversial of the Narnia books. Many people who don't like the *Chronicles* say this book is the reason. The problem is racism. The background of *The Horse and His Boy* is hostility between the 'fair-skinned' Narnians and the 'dark' Calormenes – a distinction in skin colour that Lewis connects to ideas of good and evil. This conflict reappears in *The Last Battle*, the great struggle between good and evil that ends the *Chronicles*. To today's reader – and to many readers of Lewis's time as well – the portrayal of the Calormenes can appear profoundly racist. Concern about that is more than contemporary political correctness. Lewis didn't inadvertently repeat old, racist images. He dwelt on them. Even sympathetic Lewis scholars note with dismay his 'emphasis' on the racist imagery and language, and have called it 'regrettable'. This complex subject is explored in detail in an afterword to this book.

IF YOU CAN LEAD BREE TO WATER WHY WON'T HE DRINK?

HHB:
Bree

Bree may look like a horse, but he's as stubborn as a mule. He believes everything about Aslan except the fact that Aslan is real. Lewis uses him to criticize people who believe in the ideals of Christianity but don't believe Christ died and was resurrected. That's a compromise, in Lewis's view. He didn't think it was good enough. He certainly didn't believe it was enough to get into heaven.

Fortunately for Bree, Aslan makes himself visible. This is a scene Lewis drew from the Bible. In the Gospel of St John, it says that one of Jesus's disciples, Thomas, was off somewhere when Jesus came to show everyone that he had risen from the dead. Although the other disciples told Thomas the news, he didn't believe it. This is the origin of the phrase, 'a doubting Thomas'.

Lewis would have heard the name 'Bree' many times from his friend J. R. R. Tolkien. In *The Lord of the Rings*, which Tolkien read to the Inklings club over the many years he worked on it, there's a hobbit village called Bree. It's where Frodo first meets Aragorn.

But [Thomas] said to them, 'Unless I

The disciple Thomas is described in the Bible as one of a set of twins, like Cor and Corin of *The Horse and His Boy*. He is supposed to have gone to preach in India or in Parthia, an ancient country near the Caspian Sea (yes, as in *Prince Caspian*). Like the Calormenes of the *Chronicles*, the Parthians were recognized by their enemies, who included early Christians, as great riders and archers.

see the nail marks in his hands and put my finger where the nails were, and put my hand into his side, I will not believe it.'

A week later his disciples were in the house again, and Thomas was with them. Though the doors were locked, Jesus came and stood among them and said, 'Peace be with you!' Then he said to Thomas, 'Put your finger here; see my hands. Reach out your hand and put it into my side. Stop doubting and believe.'

Thomas said to him, 'My Lord and my God!'

Then Jesus told him, 'Because you have seen me, you have believed; blessed are those who have not seen and yet have believed.'

Readers who know Narnia but not Lewis's other work may think he was interested only in the moral code of his religion, not the literal truth of the Gospel's supernatural events. That would be common for a twentieth-century author. For Lewis, however, the essence of Christianity was the supernatural elements, which for him proved the existence of God.

As Bree will learn, even horses go to heaven in Narnia, but they have to believe first.

WHY DOES SHASTA GO WITH THE FLOW?

Shasta's story goes back to the days when literature was carved on stone tablets. Yet as ancient as it is, the best way to understand it is to look at it through modern eyes.

WATER, WATER, EVERYWHERE

Shasta's childhood is a story used all over the world to explain the origins of mythic heroes. A prince is hidden, often by a journey down a river or over an ocean, because of a prophecy; then he's raised humbly, without knowing his identity, before going on to his great destiny.

More than four thousand years ago, that kind of story was told about King Sargon of Akkad, a land in the Middle East. Sargon's mother puts him in a basket, and he floats down the Euphrates river until he is found by a man named Akki. He is raised as an ordinary boy, and taught to be a gardener. He eventually becomes a great king.

Shasta's name comes fom the Russian word *tshastal*, meaning 'white' or 'pure'. His Narnian name, 'Cor,' means 'heart' in Latin.

In Africa, there are stories about the famous hero Mwindo. To save him from his father, a jealous chieftain, Mwindo is put in a drum that's thrown into a river. Fortunately he already has special powers and is able to escape and find his aunt, who raises him in a nearby village. When he grows up, he wants to take revenge on his father, but forgives him instead.

The mythical founders of Rome, Romulus and Remus, sons of a king, are put in the river Tiber as infants. They are found by a wolf, who cares for them until a shepherd finds them and raises them.

In a Greek myth, a boy named Jason, who is supposed to become king, falls into danger and is hidden by a great centaur, Chiron. Eventually he takes the throne.

In the Bible, baby Moses, born a Hebrew slave in Egypt, is put in a basket and floated down a river to spare him from Pharaoh's law that all Hebrew boys are to be killed. Moses is discovered by Pharaoh's daughter and raised as a member of Pharaoh's household. When he grows up, he leads a slave revolt.

How can all these myths sound the same? Scholars are divided on the reason. Some believe a single myth was spread through the telling, sometimes being applied to heroes that already existed. Other scholars say common

Whether or not the legend of Sargon's birth is true, he was a real person, not just a mythical hero. His empire is the first in recorded history. It stretched from the Persian Gulf to what is now the Mediterranean shore of Turkey.

Cyrus the Great, another real king whose story has become entangled with ancient legends, ruled Persia in the sixth century BC.

human feelings or experiences led to different versions appearing independently. They believe myths exist to explain earthly existence, or at least make us feel better about it. For example, according to this theory, all societies have stories about an afterlife because humans have always feared death.

A FAMILY AFFAIR

For those who believe myths like these arise from common experience, there's a clever insight from one of Sigmund Freud's students, Otto Rank (1884–1939). Rank believed that the experience behind all these stories about the birth of heroes is the trauma of childbirth, followed by certain inevitable moments in early childhood. The basket in which the baby is placed is the womb; the river is the mother's birth canal. When children are young, they see their parents as all-powerful, but in time parents become more real, and children see their flaws and resent them. The children then imagine that these parents are mere accidents, and that the real, ideal parents are elsewhere. Mixed in with this theory is the observation that children may see fathers as tyrannical, so some of the mythical fathers are tyrants. But by fantasizing about a reconciliation with the fantasy father (as Shasta enjoys), or

The legends of Mwindo come from the Nyanga people, in the region near Kinshasa, the capital of the Democratic Republic of Congo. Mwindo is a special kind of hero: more often funny than serious. He's as mischievous as any of the great trickster gods, like Hermes of Greek myth (Mercury to the Romans), Loki of Norse legends, or Raven in Native American tales from the Pacific North-west.

overthrowing him, it's possible to bear the suffering.

Freud himself had a different explanation for these myths. He didn't agree about the importance of birth trauma. He believed the story was the result of children creating fictional parents towards whom they can express feelings they might not be able to express towards their real parents.

Freud and Rank are famous for disagreeing on many things by the end of their careers, but they agree that this myth begins with a child's natural self-absorption and self-importance. To mature, a child has to pass through these stages of fantasy and leave them behind.

Lewis had a completely different explanation for the hero myths, but he arrived at the same conclusion.

CIRCULAR ARGUMENTS

Lewis believed there was a psychological side to these myths, a common human feeling that caused them to appear independently in many parts of the world. He thought they all related to a single event – one which had yet to happen, and which the common feelings were anticipating.

Because the myths have parallels to the stories of Christ, Lewis believed they came

Some of the many other heroes who fit the pattern: Oedipus, Perseus and Heracles of Greek myth; the Hindu god Krishna; Gilgamesh of Sumerian and Babylonian legend.

from feelings that God put inside humankind. He believed God wanted people to have an idea of what was to come. Lewis's theory was that this feeling led ancient peoples to tell stories like Christ's even before Christ lived. To go back to the example above, people believed stories about an afterlife have always existed because God has always given people a sense that there is one. This is Lewis's version of what Robert Louis Stevenson called 'nameless longings'. Lewis believed the similar myths about the birth of heroes are God-given premonitions of the birth of Christ.

That doesn't mean Shasta is supposed to be Christ. Lewis gives Shasta the biography of a classical hero, but he wants Shasta to be the symbol of the opposite. Shasta has to learn that he's not important in the grand scheme of the world. Self-centredness, Lewis said, was a sin, 'the basic sin', the 'sin of Satan' (*Mere Christianity*, p.43). He believed there could be no maturity, and no religious understanding, without the loss of self. Even for princes.

As an infant, the Trojan prince Paris was sent from Troy and left on a mountain to die because a prophecy said he would be the city's ruin. Saved by a shepherd and eventually restored to the royal family, he fulfilled the prophecy when he started the Trojan War by kidnapping the wife of King Menelaus of Sparta.

WHAT'S THE KNIGHT'S TALE?

At the end of *The Horse and His Boy*, Shasta reveals a wish to Aravis. He wants to know the name of the knight who saved his life when he was an infant. The knight guided the boat on which Shasta was sent from danger, and Shasta finally understands that the knight 'kept me alive and starved himself to do it' (*The Horse and His Boy*, ch.14). We're supposed to think the wish is a sign that Shasta is finally thinking of others.

Unfortunately, Lewis doesn't answer the question. He makes Aravis guess that it's one of the times when Aslan won't tell one person's story to another. Shasta lets it drop.

Why suggest Shasta would lose interest so quickly, now that he has the power to reward the knight's family? Isn't it worth at least asking Aslan? A knight who dies to keep an oath – so important in Narnia – deserves more from a new prince.

The name Aravis comes from the ancient Greek word 'arabis', meaning an Arab woman. (A modern Greek version of the word has become a strong derogatory term.)

Joshua Kronengold, a member of the Mytho-poeic Society, which studies works by authors like Lewis and J. R. R. Tolkien, has discovered the source of the knight in a play by Shakespeare. In *The Winter's Tale* (1610), a baby girl is saved by Lord Antigonus, who takes her by boat to a foreign land where she is found by a shepherd. Scholars believe Shakespeare added a chaperone to the old story of a hidden baby to make his play more believable.

Shakespeare based *The Winter's Tale* on a romance called *Pandosto* (1588), by Robert Greene. There is no character like Antigonus in Greene's story.

Once the baby was safe with the shepherd, Shakespeare had to make Antigonus, who knows the baby's identity, disappear. (The king who orders the baby out of the kingdom has a change of heart, so Shakespeare couldn't make it easy for the baby to be found.) Shakespeare's solution, some scholars say, was a sly joke. In Shakespeare's time, theatres were also used for another popular entertainment, bear-baiting, in which dogs were set loose to fight a bear. Shakespeare wrote a stage direction for Antigonus's final scene that has now become famous: 'Exit, pursued by a bear'.

THE ONLY TRUE BEGETTER
Despite this borrowing, Lewis wasn't a great

fan of Shakespeare. *The Winter's Tale*, however, was special to him. It was one of only three Shakespeare plays he liked, he once told a friend. At the end of the story, a queen who seems to have died earlier in the play miraculously comes back to life. When he was young he thought the scene was 'silly', but later it 'overwhelmed' him. 'Shakespeare (probably unconsciously) is able to give us an image of the whole idea of resurrection,' he said (*Letters of C. S. Lewis*, p.420).

Lewis admitted he was reading too much into the play. He didn't care. As he told a friend, he had come to a point in life where any new play or book had meaning to him only if it reminded him of myths he already wanted to see. (He was all of thirty-two years old at the time.)

But given Lewis's feelings about the play, surely he would have made Aslan tell the story of the Narnian knight whose Shakespearean kin swore this oath:

> *King Leontes*: What will you adventure
> To save this brat's life?
> *Antigonus*: Anything, my lord,
> That my ability may undergo
> And nobleness impose.

The other plays Lewis listed with *The Winter's Tale* as favourites were *The Tempest* and *A Midsummer Night's Dream*, both of which are literally fairy tales. As he grew older he once again became fascinated by a fourth, *Hamlet*, that had been his favourite when he was very young. Prince Rilian of *The Silver Chair* was inspired by the Prince of Denmark. (See p.157.)

At least thus much:
I'll pawn the little blood which I have left
To save the innocent.

(Act II, sc. iii)

What could be more in keeping with Aslan's and Lewis's philosophy?

WHICH WAY TO NARNIA?

HHB: Northerness

Bree rallies everyone with the cheer, 'To Narnia and the North!' That was a rallying cry for Lewis too, one that began as a feeling and became an idea. Lewis called it 'Northerness'.

The feeling came from a Henry Wadsworth Longfellow poem about a Norse myth. Lewis read the poem when he was young, and a few lines were 'like a voice from far more distant regions'.

> I heard a voice that cried,
> Balder the Beautiful
> Is dead, is dead –

'Instantly I was uplifted into huge regions of northern sky,' Lewis recalled. 'Cold, spacious, severe, pale and remote.' Those aren't words from travel brochures, but Lewis wanted to

Balder is the Norse god of light, peace and beauty. He is a generous god. Only the trickster god Loki dislikes him. Loki learns Balder's one weakness, mistletoe, and arranges for him to be killed with an arrow of it. But the legends say Balder will one day come back to life.

As Paul F. Ford and others have noted, when Aslan turns Prince Rabadash into a donkey in *The Horse and His Boy*, it's an allusion to the Bible story of Nebuchadnezzar (c. 605–562 BC), the king who made Babylon (near what's now Baghdad, Iraq) a great city. He was too proud of his works, so God turned him into a beast with feathers and claws that 'ate grass like oxen'. Given a second chance, he learned to obey God.

experience the North 'with almost sickening intensity' (*Surprised by Joy*, p.23).

From this moment came a lifelong fascination with Norse myth: Icelandic sagas, the operas of Richard Wagner, tales of Siegfried and dragons. This isn't as strange as it sounds. Biographer A. N. Wilson offers the observation, 'In the decades before the First World War, when a Victorian passion for all things Teutonic and Northern still gripped the British middle class, it is hardly surprising that all this should have come Lewis's way' (*C. S. Lewis: A Biography*, p.29). But as Wilson also acknowledges, a passion for Richard Wagner in a teenage boy is slightly unusual. Lewis was lucky enough to learn that a neighbour, Arthur Greeves, shared his interest in Norse myth. Greeves became a lifelong friend. Later, at Oxford, Lewis would learn J. R. R. Tolkien adored the same stories. (See p.68.)

TWILIGHT OF THE GODS

An obvious question is, if Lewis loved this feeling about the icy north, why is it a bad thing that in *The Lion, the Witch and the Wardrobe* Jadis wants a permanent winter in Narnia? Lewis's feelings were mixed.

On the one hand, he loved the Norse myths for their tales of great heroism and for their connection to death. Even in Norse legends, the extreme north is a wasteland, the land of the dead. Witches come from the frozen north. That was part of the inspiration for Jadis and the first, frozen Narnia we see in *The Lion, the Witch and the Wardrobe*. It's also a source for the the Green Witch and her northern castle in *The Silver Chair*. The owls and dwarves in *The Silver Chair* talk about 'those Northern Witches' (*The Silver Chair*, ch.15).

Intellectually, however, Lewis saw Norse legends as a stepping stone to Christianity. The phrase in the Longfellow poem that captured his imagination, about the death of the god Balder, is part of the story of the death of the whole pantheon of Norse gods – the 'twilight' of their domination, just before Christianity replaced them. The poem goes on:

In *Paradise Lost*, John Milton mentions witches from 'Lapland', northern Scandinavia. They're also an important part of Philip Pullman's *His Dark Materials*.

> I saw the pallid corpse
> Of the dead sun
> Borne through the Northern sky.
> Blasts from Niffelheim
> Lifted the sheeted mists
> Around him as he passed.
> . . . So perish the old Gods!
> But out of the sea of Time
> Rises a new land of song,

Fairer than the old.
Over its meadows green
Walk the young bards and sing.
      . . . Sing no more,
O ye bards of the North,
Of Vikings and of Jarls!
Of the days of Eld
Preserve the freedom only,
Not the deeds of blood!

Chinese legends tell of Xuanwu, a 'Dark Warrior' from the North. Xuanwu, an entwined tortoise and snake, symbolizes winter.

Lewis, like Longfellow, enjoyed those deeds of blood, even if it was from a safe distance of a few hundred years. He still sang of them, literally, in raucous gatherings of friends. But he follows Longfellow's advice in the *Chronicles*, giving Narnia the idea of freedom without the extreme, severe, deathly Northerness that fascinated him personally.

PRINCE CASPIAN:
LEWIS'S THOUGHTS

PC:
Introduction

In the middle of the *Chronicles* – according to the reading order now suggested by Lewis's publishers – readers come to three stories in a row that are linked by the adventurous and virtuous Caspian. He is Prince Caspian in the book of that name, then King Caspian X in *The Voyage of the 'Dawn Treader'* and *The Silver Chair*.

It's important to remember the difference between the original order in which the books were published and the order for reading that was suggested later. The numbers on the spines of current volumes give the impression of a clear progression that wasn't in Lewis's mind as he was writing. And Lewis hadn't imagined the later books, such as *The Last Battle*, when he began plotting the stories that followed *The Lion, the Witch and the Wardrobe*. We know now that the series ends with Lewis's version of Armageddon, the great battle

Mary Clare Havard, to whom *Prince Caspian* was dedicated, was the daughter of Lewis's close friend and doctor, Robert 'Humphrey' Havard.

between good and evil described at the end of the New Testament. But Lewis didn't know that. He hadn't planned a clear path through Bible stories. As originally published, the *Chronicles* were a series of stand-alone adventures with recurring characters.

The adventures were created in a casual way. In notebooks, Lewis refers to various plots and ideas that interested him: two children on a ship, pursued by enemies; a picture that acts as a portal to Narnia; an 'ordinary fairy tale' with a king, queen and court, 'into which erupts a child from our world'; a story in which the villains are human 'tyrants' (*C. S. Lewis: A Companion and Guide*, p.403). The ship and picture ended up in *The Voyage of the 'Dawn Treader'*. The story of men as tyrants, which in note form also mentioned a 'Dwarf', became *Prince Caspian*, which features the half-Dwarf Dr Cornelius.

These are adventures with added symbolism, not symbols dressed up for make-believe. In *Prince Caspian*, it's easy to imagine the religious elements are just atmosphere. There are plenty of stories about undeserving kings who have taken thrones from the rightful heirs. Not all of them mention religion. Of course for Lewis the religious element took centre stage. In his story, the false king and the

The name 'Caspian' had been in Lewis's head a long time. In an unfinished narrative poem, from twenty-five years before he started to write *Prince Caspian*, the name belongs to an older half-sister of the central characters – one of whom, a boy, is named 'Jardis'. (See p.192.)

Telmarines represent a corruption of the early true religion of Narnia established by Aslan. Caspian isn't merely restoring the proper line of kings. He's restoring the old religion. But he's still a prince, and this volume is still a fairy tale.

Prince Caspian is the only Narnia book with a subtitle. 'The Return to Narnia' refers to it being the second Narnia book Lewis wrote.

WHAT'S THE TWIST IN REEPICHEEP'S TALE?

Heavy lies the head that wears the crown. Caspian and the Pevensies constantly wonder if they're doing the right thing. Their duties change without warning, and it would offend Aslan if they shied from the big decisions.

Reepicheep is luckier. He can trust their authority when it comes to the complicated questions and live by a simple code himself.

If all the characters acted like Reepicheep, there would be no *Chronicles*. He doesn't doubt. He doesn't ask for proof about Aslan. He doesn't lose faith. He's the gallant knight of the sort Lewis adored in the tales of King Arthur. He accepts the word of Aslan and the word of his kings without question. Despite being mistreated by Eustace in *The Voyage of the 'Dawn Treader'*, Reepicheep comforts him. He does it because it is the right thing to do. Whether or not he wants to do it, and how

'Thou wilt be as valiant as the wrathful dove or most magnanimous mouse' – Falstaff, the cowardly buffoon, recruiting a soldier in Shakespeare's *Henry IV, Part 2* (Act III, Sc. ii).

Eustace treated him in the past, aren't considerations. He even sticks to the code when princes and kings hesitate. He won't let Caspian abdicate the throne to join him on the journey to World's End in *The Voyage of the 'Dawn Treader'* because that would mean Caspian is breaking an oath.

A LITTLE GOES A LONG WAY

Would Reepicheep be so admirable if he were a prince or a king? Maybe not. He might be a bore, except as comic relief. What makes him charming – and fearsome – is the contrast between his tiny stature and his huge heart. Don't we all love small heroes? A few years before Lewis began the *Chronicles*, readers fell for E. B. White's *Stuart Little* (1945). American readers still marvel at Amos – as in 'a mouse' – in Robert Lawson's 1939 delight, *Ben and Me*. (Amos lives in Ben Franklin's coonskin cap and is the real brain behind the first American genius.) Several mice, like Martin the Warrior, are heroes of Brian Jacques's Redwall books. Michael Hoeye's recent Hérmux Tantamoq adventures, starting with *Time Stops for No Mouse* (2002), are every bit as appealing.

Lewis makes one of the oldest mouse stories part of the *Chronicles* – with a twist. In *The Lion, the Witch and the Wardrobe*, mice

In one of the stories set in the imaginary land of Boxen that Lewis wrote as a child, Sir Peter Mouse, the gallant sword-wielding precursor to Reepicheep, wakes up one morning, after having what he thought was a nightmare, to discover his tail 'mystereousely missing' (*Boxen*, p.35). Another mouse had cut it off during the night. (See also p.20.)

chew away the ropes that held Aslan bound during the execution at the Stone Table. Anyone who has read Aesop's fables will notice the allusion to Aesop's 'The Lion and the Mouse'. In that old story, a lion wakes up one day to find a group of mice playing on him. He catches one, but lets it go. The next day, when the lion is caught in a net, the mice save him by gnawing the cords.

In Lewis's version, the mice help the lion without having been helped first. That makes Aslan the one who can grant a favour in return. In *Prince Caspian* he restores Reepicheep's tail.

The Narnian twist on Aesop's lesson echoes the warning in the Bible's Book of Matthew: 'What you do to the least of them, you do to me.'

Very little is known for certain about Aesop, a freed Greek slave who lived about 620–560 BC. If all the stories are true, he advised great kings and had dramatic adventures.

His fables come to us through other writers. Plato said his mentor Socrates put the stories into verse while in prison, about a century after Aesop died.

WHY DOES BACCHUS HAVE SO MANY NAMES?

Lucy and Susan can tell at a glance Bacchus is the kind of boy their parents wouldn't want them to meet.

In real life two adventurous girls might want to get closer to someone who looks like a lot of trouble and a lot of fun. In Narnia they're safe from him – and from themselves. They can only wonder about him, from a distance. Why is he surrounded by dancers? Why do the dancers call him by so many names?

The names hint at Bacchus's popularity. Lewis mentions three: Bromios, Bassareus, and the Ram. That's only the beginning. There are dozens, and a good story is attached to nearly every one. Bacchus is actually the god of wine in Greek and Roman mythology. He was known for wild adventures in faraway places.

Here's what Lucy and Susan were missing, and why Lewis thought Bacchus was a worthy

Because Bacchus appeared in Greek legends after the other Olympians, some scholars believe the Greeks adopted him from eastern mythology. This may explain why myths about him often occur in foreign lands.

123

friend of Aslan, even if he is a bit of a juvenile delinquent.

It's My Party and I'll Cry if I Want To

Bacchus is a name used primarily by the Romans. (The Romans adopted Bacchus, like the other Olympians, from the Greeks.) It's a Latinized version of one his oldest names, the Greek *Bakchos*. It means 'Crier', as in a loud call or a cry of joy. Bromios has a similar meaning: 'the Thunderer' or 'the Shouter'.

Lucy and Susan hear the dancers call out 'Euan, euan, eu-oi-oi-oi', which was the cry at wild parties in classical times. It refers to another name attached to Bacchus. *Eu* in Greek means 'good'. The name Bacchus Euan would be something like Good Ol' Bacchus or Bacchus the Great.

The common British name Euan seems to have a different source. It's Scottish, and means roughly 'born of the yew tree'. (Yews are said to have great strength and even magical powers, and live thousands of years.)

Be Careful What You Wish For

Bacchus got the name Dithyrambos, 'he of the double door', from the way he was born.

Bacchus's mother was the mortal Semele. His father was the god Zeus. When Zeus's wife, the goddess Hera, found out that Semele was pregnant, she was furious. As revenge, she made Semele doubt Zeus's affection. Semele became jealous that Zeus always appeared to her as a mortal, rather than as a god, so she tricked him into showing himself in his true Olympian form. Unfortunately, his thunder and lightning burnt her to a crisp. Zeus rescued the unborn Bacchus from the ashes, then sewed Bacchus into his thigh until the boy was ready to be born. So Bacchus came into the world through two doors.

(Apparently 'Bakhos' itself is a pun in ancient Greek, and means the 'Scion' or 'Offspring' of the god Zeus.)

Go Tell It On the Mountain

In ancient Greece, and to modern scholars, the name by which Bacchus is best known is 'Dionysus'. This name is also related to the story of Semele and Hera.

Hera was happy that Semele was gone, but didn't like the idea of Zeus having a son by another wife. Zeus knew she felt that way, so he hid the infant. Hera found Bacchus with a mortal family, and caused so much trouble that Zeus gave Bacchus to the nymphs on Mount Nysa, far from Greece. The name Dionysus means 'God of Nysa'.

This episode also explains the name 'the Ram' that Lewis mentions. While on Nysa, Bacchus was disguised by Zeus as a goat.

No one knows precisely where this ancient Mount Nysa was. Depending on the legend, it's in what's now Arabia, North Africa, or eastern Turkey.

When Bacchus grew up he discovered how to grow grapes and make wine. He was known as Dionysos Lênaios or 'Dionysos of the Winepress'. Naturally, as the god of wine, he became a party god. He was called Euhastêr or Euhios, meaning 'The Reveller'. As Edmund said, he was 'a chap who might do anything absolutely anything' (*Prince Caspian*, ch.11). Wild parties were known as Bacchanalias or Bacchanals. They still are.

The Athenians celebrated the festivals of Bacchus with great splendour, and the Romans followed their lead. Like the celebration Lucy and Susan witnessed in Narnia, some of these were Girls' Nights Out. Few men, if any, were invited. The 'fierce, madcap girls' at the party in Narnia (*Prince Caspian*, ch.14) were known in Greece by the name Lewis mentions, Maenads, meaning 'the raving ones'. They appear often in classical art, pictured crowned with vine leaves, clothed in skins and dancing wildly.

When Roman Bacchanals were opened to men, celebrations took place up to five times a month. Authorities became concerned by the rowdiness, and also feared (perhaps unjustly) that crimes and political conspiracies were

In mythology, Bacchus's friend Silenus is as he appears in *Prince Caspian*: a fat, old, jolly drunk. He rides a donkey or is carried by friends. In many legends he's Bacchus's mentor, and is often a Satyr, like Mr Tumnus.

being planned at the parties. In 186 BC the Roman Senate banned Bacchanals. Citizens weren't quick to obey the law. Still, the Senate was luckier than a king in a famous Greek play. *The Bacchae*, written by Euripedes in about 406 BC, shows the festivals didn't bring out the best in everyone. When King Pentheus of Thebes bans the worship of Bacchus, the god lures him into the woods, where the Maenads tear the king apart.

RSVP

It may seem odd for Lewis, a Christian, to say a party like the one in *Prince Caspian*, led by the pagan god Bacchus, would help restore the 'true' religion of Narnia. Early Christianity was hostile to the religion of Greece and Rome, and to the nature worship that Bacchus represents. That attitude still exists. Lewis didn't accept that view. He believed that many pagan rituals expressed humankind's desire to make contact with the divine. He believed those rituals were meant to bring the same sort of joy he sought from religion. Although at times his attitude towards non-Christians of his own era was condescension or even ridicule, he didn't discount the religious sincerity of people who lived before Christianity.

The story of King Midas begins with Silenus. Midas took care of a lost and drunken Silenus, earning a wish from Dionysus. He asked that everything he touched be turned into gold. But he couldn't eat because his food became gold, and he turned his daughter to gold by accident. Dionysus let him wash away the power in a river. The gold king in the Deathwater Island lake in *The Voyage of the 'Dawn Treader'* comes from this myth.

He also didn't think a regular drink or two or three, along with loud, bawdy songs, disqualified anyone from heaven. Lewis had more than a little bit of Bacchus in him. Bacchus belongs in Narnia for that reason alone.

'Bacchae' was another name for the Maenads. They were also called the Bassarids, because Bacchus wore a fox skin (*bassaris*). This outfit explains the name Bassareus, which Lewis mentions.

This ancient drawing refers to a story in which Dionysus is kidnapped by pirates. The pirates realize who he is when he makes vines grow all over the ship. They jump overboard in fear. Dionysus saves them by turning them into dolphins, and the Greek word for dolphin becomes another of his names: *Delphis*.

WHY DID ONLY LUCY SEE WHAT LUCY SAW?

Nobody's perfect. How else to explain the sudden loss of faith by Peter and Susan and Edmund? Lucy tells them she has seen Aslan at the top of a mountain, leading the way, but despite all they've been through, they doubt her.

You can take it as a flaw in their characters, as many readers do. Others, myself included, take it as a flaw in them *as* characters. By the time we read *Prince Caspian*, we know them well enough to know they wouldn't casually forsake Aslan. It doesn't ring true when it happens. Though anything is possible, there's no foreshadowing of their change of heart, or later explanation for it.

This is a matter of taste. There's no sense arguing for it or against it. However, for those who share the feeling that something isn't right here, it may be useful to consider Lewis's intentions in *Prince Caspian*.

When Aslan tells Lucy she is a 'lioness', he's echoing a line in the Bible about the mother of the righteous (Ezekiel 19:2).

129

After the Pevensies wake up – from both sleep and their ignorance – a morning star, Aravir, appears. This is an allusion to Christ, called in the Bible 'the bright and morning star' (Revelations 22:16). Lewis took the name Aravir from a king in *The Lord of the Rings*. It means 'King of Men', which fits Lewis's use too.

Tolkien's story also had a morning star, Eärendil, that was the herald of a saviour.

For much of his life, Lewis tried to balance the rational side of his personality, which sometimes appears to have demanded a logical theory for everything, big and small, with his deep belief in something invisible. He knew that at any given moment in time, religion requires a leap of faith. He knew it can be hard to make that leap when the religion requires belief in events that occurred thousands of years before. Before his religious revival, he thought of Christ as too distant to be real to him. Christ might have been a good example of the virtuous life, but to actually believe in the facts of Christ's life as described in the gospels was too much for Lewis.

This personal question for Lewis is an important part of *Prince Caspian*. Paul F. Ford, author of the *Companion to Narnia*, says the story asks, 'What does the effect of the passage of time have on the reality and experience of faith?' (*The C. S. Lewis Readers' Encyclopedia*, p.337). In the book, Narnia is feeling the effects of time. The Golden Age of Narnia and the rule of the Pevensies is too long past to feel convincing. Worse, the Telmarines, who came to Narnia from our world, brought scepticism with them.

To make his point, Lewis wanted his main

characters to experience the same loss of faith. Theoretically, this is smart storytelling. If the main characters merely learn that Narnians as a whole have lost their faith, it doesn't mean as much to readers. It's a fact of the story, not something emotional. Readers feel what the main characters feel.

In practical terms, as a way to tell this particular story, Lewis may not have made the best choice. To me, it seems out of character for them. They've already learned not to lose faith in Aslan. Although their flawed human nature often leads them to do things that upset Aslan, and Lewis makes sure they feel bad about it and are punished, maybe this time Lewis is forcing the error so he can show the punishment.

The living forest into which Lucy wanders was also inspired in part by the living forests in the *The Lord of the Rings*. (See p.71.)

Because he wrote the *Chronicles* without a plan for all the titles, Lewis repeated himself. A few of the books have grand finales, and a few have moments when characters who know better fail Aslan. It's not always apparent, because of the changing cast of characters. In cases like this one in *Prince Caspian*, it can be very puzzling. But, to give Lewis due credit, when a reader can imagine characters acting independently of the storyteller, the storyteller has brought the characters to life.

THE VOYAGE OF THE DAWN TREADER: LEWIS'S THOUGHTS

And here we come to the last of the three *Chronicles of Narnia* . . .

No, that's not a typographical error. *The Voyage of the 'Dawn Treader'*, third of the stories Lewis wrote, was supposed to be the final volume.

Now that you know, the signs may be obvious. Reepicheep wants to journey to the Utter East – the 'Very End of the World'. At the end of the story the children encounter a lamb and fish, both of which are symbols of Christ in our world rather than Narnia. The lamb explains directly, 'This was the very reason why you were brought to Narnia, that by knowing me here for a little, you may know me better there' (*The Voyage of the 'Dawn Treader'*, ch.16).

Lewis surely wasn't referring to those symbols when he said the Christian story in the *Chronicles* is 'hidden'. The lamb and fish are

Geoffrey Barfield, dedicatee of *The Voyage of the 'Dawn Treader'*, was the foster son of Lewis's friend Owen Barfield. (Lewis had dedicated *The Lion, the Witch and the Wardrobe* to Lucy Barfield, Geoffrey's foster sister.) Lewis was also helping to pay for Geoffrey's education.

133

On his ten-year journey home from the Trojan War, Odysseus was blown by the god Poseidon throughout the Aegean and Mediterranean seas.

Poseidon was already angry with Odysseus when the journey began, because of the war. That turned to fury after Odysseus blinded Polyphemus, the monstrous Cyclops who was Poseidon's son, in order to escape Polyphemus's cave.

especially obvious references to Christianity. Christ appears as a lamb in the Bible, and is often referred to as the 'lamb of God'. Fish are also connected to Christ's story in several ways. In the New Testament's Book of Matthew, Christ feeds a large crowd with just two fish; in Mark, the disciples are called 'fishers of men'. As the *Catholic Encyclopedia* says, 'Among the symbols employed by the primitive Christians, that of the fish ranks probably first in importance.' Long ago, the letters in the Greek word for fish, *icthys*, were used to stand for the phrase *Iesous Christos Theou Yios Soter*, Greek for 'Jesus Christ, Son of God,

Saviour'. Lewis's use of these obvious symbols is a sign that he thought *The Voyage of the 'Dawn Treader'* would be the last Narnia book.

The story begins on a different note: high adventure. Pirates, dragons, treasure and not one but *two* narrow escapes. Just as theatrical, perhaps, but less symbolic. Lewis's very first notes for the book refer to a story that would give readers the feeling of sailing to dangerous islands with Odysseus, or sailing with St Brendan to magical lands no one else had ever seen. That's still the most important part of the book.

It's probably not important that in many

Though his legend has a touch of the fantastic, St Brendan was a real person. An Irish monk, he lived from 484 to 577. He was known as 'Brendan the Voyager' for his attempt to sail to an earthly paradise mentioned in legends. From the descriptions of his journey, some people claim that he discovered North America.

Jonathan Usher of the University of Edinburgh points out that Lewis relied on the tales of Ulysses in Dante Alighieri's *Inferno* more than Homer's version. Lewis adapted several incidents and speeches, giving them all an appropriate twist: while Ulysses heads west, towards human civilization, Reepicheep fares better, because he's travelling to the east, towards the source of religious enlightenment.

spots Lewis writes as though it's his last chance to express an opinion about targets like modern parents or the government. Younger readers aren't meant to understand that he's writing on two levels. When they hear Caspian's frustrated cry that he's 'had enough of governors' (*The Voyage of the 'Dawn Treader'*, ch.4), they take it at face value: the governors in the story are bad. They don't know that Lewis wasn't overly fond of democracy. Of course young readers laugh when Caspian sneers at the words 'progress' and 'development' (*The Voyage of the 'Dawn Treader'*, ch.4). Those are dull words that have nothing to do with pirates and heroism. The adult reader sees that Lewis is sneering too, not just because plans for progress so often go awry, but because, as Caspian makes clear, they're bad goals from the start. That's Lewis: he romanticized the past and was often cranky about the present. He used the term 'chronological snobbery' to describe a preference for the present over the past. Yet he could be accused of reverse chronological snobbery.

Narnia fans know that the destinations, whether frivolous or serious, aren't what matters in *The Voyage of the 'Dawn Treader'*. The important thing is the thrilling journey.

WHY IS EUSTACE PAINED BY A BRACELET?

Whats so bad about being a dragon? You can fly. People don't bother you very often. When they do, you can snort fire at them. Anyone who has commuted to work or school on London's Tube would think twice before passing up those powers.

Unfortunately for Eustace, there's a catch. It might have been fine if he'd simply fallen asleep on the dragon's hoard and awakened to discover his new self. But he's wearing a gold bracelet that is much too small for his new body. The pain quickly becomes unbearable.

That's like another tale from the underground, but not London's. It's from a Scandinavian myth that Lewis had adored since he was not much older than Eustace.

SLEEPING BEAUTY

In Scandinavian myths, hoards of treasures are often guarded by dragons. Those hoards were

The image of Eustace having his ugly skin peeled off to reveal a new, infant-like skin, and then being thrown into the large bathing well, is an intentional religious symbol. Eustace is being reborn and baptized, standing naked before Aslan.

About a dozen
years before
Lewis wrote *The
Voyage of the
'Dawn Treader'*,
Lewis's friend
J. R. R. Tolkien
told the story of
Bilbo Baggins's
discovery of a
dragon's hoard
and a magic ring
in *The Hobbit*
(1937). Bilbo's
ring wasn't very
evil in the
original edition.
Tolkien later
revised the
book, restoring
the original
Norse theme to
support the
premise of *The
Lord of the
Rings* – that the
ring must be
destroyed.

often burial mounds, and dragons were sometimes said to be reincarnated from a corpse laid on top of them.

A story about a dragon's hoard in the collection of Norse tales called the *Volsunga Saga* is the basis for Eustace's story. The composer Richard Wagner turned the German version of it into an opera, the *Ring Cycle*, which Lewis first heard on one of his father's gramophone records. This story was one reason for Lewis's lifelong devotion to Norse myth.

According to the legend, three Norse gods are walking through the forest one day when they see an otter eating a salmon. One of the gods, Loki, throws a stone that kills the otter, then takes both the otter and the fish as his prize. That night, stopping at the house of a dwarf, the gods learn Loki had killed one of the dwarf's three sons, whose name was Ottir and who had been in animal form so he could fish.

The dwarf demands that the gods repay him with a huge amount of gold. Loki decides to steal the gold from another dwarf, Andvari, who is almost infinitely rich. Andvari has a magic gold ring that makes other gold rings.

Reluctantly, Andvari tells Loki to take all the gold – except the magic ring. Naturally,

Loki wants the magic one too. Andvari can't stop him, so he puts a curse on the ring. Tragedy will come to any mortal who wears it.

Loki gives Ottir's father all the gold, including the magic ring. The curse soon begins its work. One of the dwarf's other sons, Fafnir, is overcome by greed. He kills his father to get the ring. Then he drives his remaining brother away. Finally alone with the gold, Fafnir is happy. In Wagner's opera he says, 'I have and I hold. Let me slumber.' He falls asleep on the gold and turns into a dragon. As if that's not bad enough – Eustace would think it is – Fafnir's brother sends a warrior named Sigurd after the ring, and Sigurd slays Fafnir.

The difference between Fafnir's fate and Eustace's goes back to an aspect of Norse myth that interested Lewis from the beginning: the passing from the Norse gods to Christianity. In the original version, Fafnir pays for his greed and his violence with his life. Eustace is forgiven and given a second chance.

Tolkien turned the dwarf Andvari from the original legend into the corrupted hobbit Gollum of *The Lord of the Rings*.

WHY DID THE DARK ISLAND DISAPPEAR TWICE?

VDT:
Dark Island

After *The Voyage of the 'Dawn Treader'* was published, Lewis made a revision to account for something important to him. You wouldn't know it from reading the current editions. The change was made only in old American printings, and in recent years the original text was restored. It's almost as if the revision never happened.

Given the nature of Lewis's worry, that makes a strange kind of sense.

DREAM A LITTLE DREAM OF ME

Lewis had awful dreams in childhood. There was no obvious explanation, which only made things worse. Even as an adult he had vivid, terrifying memories of those dreams. His anxieties were one reason for creating the Dark Island in *The Voyage of the 'Dawn Treader'*.

The Dark Island isn't really a piece of land. It's a black mist that only appears to be an

Aslan's appearance as an albatross in the frightening episode of the Dark Island follows the sailor's legend: an albatross is a good omen. To kill one, as in Samuel Taylor Coleridge's long poem 'The Rime of the Ancient Mariner' (1798), is said to be a sin.

Reepicheep says if Caspian tries to give up the throne to follow him to the World's End, he will bind Caspian to the mast of the 'Dawn Treader'. Edmund recalls a similar scene in *The Odyssey*. Odysseus wants to hear the Sirens, creatures who sing beautiful songs to lure sailors on to rocks. To do it, he orders the men to tie him to the mast of his ship and to plug their ears until they've passed the Sirens.

island at first, but in fact is just a menacing void. Nothing can be seen, but there are awful sounds. The ship's crew hears a voice in the darkness, begging to be saved from the horror. The crew pulls on board a terrified stranger – later we learn he is Lord Rhoop – who tells them this is the place where dreams come true. He's not talking about happy dreams.

In the original version of the story, as soon as the sailors are past the Dark Island they say it was just an illusion. 'I reckon we've made pretty good fools of ourselves,' Rynelf says (*The Magician's Nephew*, ch.12). Some time after the book's British publication, Lewis came to regret that reaction. He didn't want readers to feel foolish for being terrified by their own inexplicable night fears. Given the opportunity to change the text for the American edition, he deleted Rynelf's conclusion and made a few other changes to let young readers know the Dark Island really exists in Narnia. Being frightened was bad enough, he figured. Feeling foolish or just plain insane would be much worse.

It makes perfect sense, given his own experience. But for some reason the American edition now reads like the British, which was never altered. Once again, the Dark Island seems to have disappeared completely.

WHAT'S THE STORY IN THE MAGICIAN'S BOOK?

Every good magician has enough spells to fill a book. Coriakin's book has something more. When the Dufflepuds are tired of being invisible and ask Lucy to read Coriakin's book to find a visibility spell, she comes across some strange magic.

GETTING FRESH

The 'spell for refreshment' in the elaborately illustrated book is three pages long, and 'more like a story than a spell'. Although Lucy's 'living in the story' rather than merely reading it, almost as soon as she's finished she forgets all of it except for a few fragments. A cup. A tree. A sword. A green hill (*The Voyage of the 'Dawn Treader'*, ch.10). Those are all symbols from the story of Christ's death and resurrection.

A cup. At the last supper before his crucifixion, Jesus drank from a chalice or cup. And stained glass church windows throughout

In some legends, 'Holy Grail' refers to Jesus's cup at the Last Supper. In others, that cup is called the Holy Chalice, while the Grail is the cup that caught Jesus's blood when he was on the Cross. In both, the cups are prized relics, and have been hunted for more than a thousand years.

Europe show Joseph of Arimathea and Mary Magdalene, disciples of Jesus, catching his blood in a cup while he is on the Cross.

A tree. The tree is a symbol of the Cross. Some Bible texts refer to Jesus being 'hanged on a tree' (Acts 5:30). There are people who take this literally; others say it's a question of translating old texts, and that a wooden cross would have been described with the same word. For Lewis, in the *Chronicles*, the image is what mattered.

A sword. Christ was pierced in the side by a sword during the crucifixion, according to the Gospel of St John. (Some accounts refer to a lance, but the image of a sword is a more memorable illustration for Coriakin's book.)

A green hill. Calvary, the hill on which Jesus died, is often referred to as a green hill, most notably in the popular hymn 'There Is A Green Hill Far Away'. Lewis knew that young British readers of the *Chronicles*, at least in his time, would encounter this hymn soon if they hadn't already.

The three sleeping kings on Ramandu's Island, under an enchantment because one of them touched the Stone Knife, come from Arthurian legends. In those old stories, touching the lance used in Christ's crucifixion begins a similar enchantment. Other legends tell of kings who guard the Holy Grail.

The Silver Chair:
Lewis's Thoughts

SC:
Introduction

None of Lewis's many books before *The Lion, the Witch and the Wardrobe* were written for children. What 'drove him into the form', biographer A. N. Wilson says, was a confrontation that ended badly for Lewis. In *The Silver Chair*, Lewis brought that scene to life again. That time he gave himself the last word.

His nemesis was the philosopher Elizabeth Anscombe (1919–2001), a graduate of Oxford, who was doing postgraduate work at Cambridge when she and Lewis had a debate like the one between the Green Witch and Puddleglum. It may be hard to imagine that a formal intellectual debate would be so hurtful to Lewis, but it left Lewis distraught.

This was in 1948, when Lewis, almost fifty, had published a long list of books on religion and literature. He was enormously popular because of wartime BBC radio broadcasts of

Lewis dedicated *The Silver Chair* to Nicholas Hardie, son of Inklings member Colin Hardie.

short essays. He was one of Oxford's best known lecturers. Anscombe was a twenty-nine-year-old student. More than that, she was a woman, which at the time meant her intellect wasn't always given the credit it was due. (Not just a mistake, a huge one. As an obituary said, 'she was considered by some to be the greatest English philosopher of her generation,' who 'helped change the course of moral philosophy'.)

Normally Lewis was an exceptionally successful debater – partly because he might say anything necessary to win an argument. But as Wilson describes it, 'Anscombe was a match for Lewis not only in mind but also in personality. She shared his taste for fisticuffs, for brutality as well as finesse in argument . . . She was quite equal to the bullying and the exploitation of the audience to which Lewis resorted when he was boxed into a corner.'

Their debate was held at the Oxford Socratic Club, founded to discuss religion. The subject was a question Lewis had raised in a book the year before. *Miracles* was an attempt to prove, with philosophical arguments, that miracles like the work of God and the birth of Christ are logical beliefs rather than just faith.

Anscombe didn't disagree with Lewis's

Is the Green Witch really Jadis in disguise? No. She's a new villain. Jadis died at the end of *The Lion, the Witch and the Wardrobe*. In Narnian time, she was still alive for the back story of *The Magician's Nephew*, but that's it.

belief in God. She was a firm believer herself. She just thought Lewis's thinking and arguments were fuzzy. They were. They also happened to attack the arguments of Anscombe's mentor, Ludwig Wittgenstein, probably the most influential philosopher of the century, and someone whose work Anscombe could explain better than anyone. Anscombe shredded Lewis, who had never before lost a Socratic Club debate.

'ONE WORD, MA'AM . . .'

For Lewis, the defeat was strangely debilitating. He told a friend 'his argument for the existence of God had been demolished'. This was an overreaction. Wilson, who is not an apologist for Lewis, sums it up sensibly: 'All that had happened, humiliating as it had been at the time, was that Lewis had been shown to have no competence to debate with a professional philopher on her own terms.' However, 'it awakened all sorts of deeply seated fears in Lewis, not least his fear of women. Once the bullying hero of the hour had been cut down to size, he became a child, a little boy who was being degraded and shaken by a figure who, in his imagination, took on witch-like dimensions . . .' (*C. S. Lewis: A Biography*).

Lewis later revised *Miracles* to account for

The Oxford University Socratic Club was founded in 1941 by Stella Aldwinkle to discuss 'the intellectual difficulties connected with religion and with Christianity in particular'. Though very religious herself, she wanted to address the arguments of atheists and agnostics. At her request, Lewis became the club's faculty adviser and president.

Anscombe's logic. But even then he didn't let the matter rest. In 1953 he presented a paper to the Socratic Club, later published as the essay 'On Obstinacy in Belief'. Anscombe may have won the logical argument, but Lewis continued to believe he was right, even if he couldn't find the right words to explain himself. It's like the retort he has Puddleglum deliver to the Green Witch on his behalf in *The Silver Chair*. 'One word, ma'am . . . one word. All you've been saying is quite right, I shouldn't wonder. [But] I'm going to live as like a Narnian as I can even if there isn't any Narnia . . .'

That might not win minds at Oxford, but it works in Narnia. Lewis makes sure Jill and Eustace respond with a cheer for 'Good old Puddleglum!' (*The Silver Chair*, ch.12).

Though he speaks for Lewis during the fight with the Green Witch, Puddleglum was actually based on Lewis's gardener, Fred Paxford, 'an inwardly optimistic, outwardly pessimistic, dear, frustrating, shrewd countryman'.

IS THE SILVER CHAIR PART OF A SET?

By the rules of 'an old folklore motif', Lewis used to tell his students, 'if you eat or sleep in the underworld you will never get back' (*Spenser's Images of Life*, p.31). Lewis was lecturing about Edmund Spenser's poem *The Faerie Queene*. In that epic, a knight almost falls into a trap like the one the Lady of the Green Kirtle sets for Prince Rilian. Both Lewis and Spenser were following a motif that goes back to classical myths.

MILES TO GO BEFORE I SLEEP

In *The Silver Chair*, the Lady of the Green Kirtle – the Green Witch – keeps Prince Rilian enchanted. Most of the time, he doesn't even know who he is. She fools him into believing he is evil and she is helping him, when the opposite is true. He isn't evil. She's holding him prisoner with her magic. In his one hour a day of sanity, he is tied to a silver chair, the

A kirtle is a long dress with a fitted bodice, usually with long sleeves, common in the Middle Ages. (A man's garment from the same period also called a kirtle was more like a tunic.)

149

Green Witch's 'vile engine of sorcery' (*The Silver Chair*, ch.11). At the end of the hour, he is under her spell again.

In *The Faerie Queene*, a hero is also offered a silver chair in the underworld. Sir Guyon, a knight who faces many temptations in the course of the epic, passes three days with Mammon, the money god. He is as much a prisoner as a guest. Mammon offers Guyon money, goods and even marriage to his daughter. But *The Faerie Queene* is an allegory, and Sir Guyon represents 'Temperance', self-restraint. He tells Mammon, 'All your idle offers I refuse. All that I need I have.'

Even then, Mammon doesn't give up. He tempts the Knight, who has not eaten or slept in three days, to eat a bit of fruit, or rest for a moment in a 'silver seat'.

Guyon refuses a final time, and Mammon frees him from the underworld. Guyon collapses from exhaustion. But he's safe. Unlike Rilian.

Mammon makes an anonymous appearance in the underground scenes of *The Silver Chair*. Lewis once said: 'Mammon is the gold-hoarding earthman of immemorial tradition, the gnome' (*The Allegory of Love*, p.312).

USED FURNITURE

An example from Greek myth shows what Lewis meant when he called the motif 'old'.

The hero Pirithous decided that he wanted to marry Persephone, who was already the wife of Hades, king of the underworld.

Pirithous and his friend Theseus decide they'll go to the underworld and tell Hades they're going to take Persephone. Instead of getting angry when they tell him their plan, Hades acts like the perfect host, offering them each a chair. But these are the Chairs of Oblivion. As soon as they sit, snakes – like the true form of the Lady of the Green Kirtle in Lewis's story – coil around their legs and hold them to the chairs. They forget who they are or why they came, and they can't move from their seats.

Theseus is lucky: when Heracles comes to the underworld for his twelfth labour, kidnapping the three-headed guard dog Cerberus, he sees Theseus and wrenches him from the chair. He is unable to free Pirithous, who is stuck for eternity.

As another Greek myth shows, a silver chair is an old tool of witches, even when not in the underworld. In *The Odyssey*, Odysseus and his men land on the island of the sorceress Circe, who uses her wand to turn Odysseus's crew into swine. Odysseus himself hasn't yet fallen under her spell when she calls him to her home.

> I fared onward to the house of Circe, and my heart was clouded with care as I walked along. When I got to the gates, I

The serpent form of the Green Witch comes from another ancient motif. Serpent women are common in myths. They appear in legends from ancient Greece and India, among other places. Ancient scholars, hearing these legends reported as facts, even recorded them in works of natural history.

stood there and called the goddess, and as soon as she heard me she came down, opened the door, and asked me to come in; so I followed her – much troubled in my mind. She set me on a richly decorated seat inlaid with silver, there was a footstool also under my feet, and she mixed a mess in a golden goblet for me to drink; but she drugged it, for she meant me mischief. When she had given it me, and I had drunk it without its charming me, she struck me with her wand. 'There now,' she cried, 'be off to the pigsty, and make your lair with the rest of them.'

As it happens, Odysseus resists her spells and Circe falls under his. But that's a different folklore motif.

Lewis felt that Circe, like Lilith, is an example of women who use femininity to achieve power over men. He believed this described women in general.

WHY CAN'T JILL REMEMBER FOUR SIMPLE SIGNS?

Why does Aslan let so many fools into Narnia? The children who visit from our world can't seem to get anything right. They release evil. They become dragons. They fall for the charms of Jadis. And Jill Pole must be the worst. All she has to do is remember four simple signs, given to her by a large talking lion who represents God. How could she possibly forget them? There's no reason given in the story. She just does.

It must be tedious for Aslan. Lewis seems to sense it's in danger of becoming tedious for the reader. 'I will not always be scolding,' Aslan practically apologizes near the end of the book (*The Silver Chair*, ch.16). There comes a point where Lewis's desire to show humankind as flawed seems to get in the way of creating characters a reader can respect. The simple answer to the question in this chapter is, there's no reason – as in, no *good* reason – why

Aslan's instruction is meant to echo the Bible: '. . . These words which I command thee shall be in thy heart: And thou shalt tell them to thy children, and thou shalt meditate upon them sitting in thy house, and walking on thy journey, sleeping and rising. . . ' (Deuteronomy. 6:6–9).

Jill can't remember the four signs.

There is, however, an observation by an accomplished Lewis scholar that offers a way to think about her mysterious incompetence, and about the *Chronicles* as a whole.

Dr Don W. King notes a connection between the seven volumes of the *Chronicles* and the seven deadly sins (pride, greed, lust, envy, gluttony, anger and sloth). 'Since Lewis so readily refers to the seven deadly sins in many of his other works, it is my contention that he may either consciously or subconsciously have emphasized one of the seven deadly sins in each one of the seven Narnian books' (*Narnia and the Seven Deadly Sins*, pp.14–19).

King acknowledges that Lewis isn't following a strict pattern. Nonetheless, here's how he sees the series:

In *The Lion, the Witch and the Wardrobe*, Edmund gets into trouble because of gluttony. A bite of Turkish Delight is all it takes to fall under Jadis's power.

In *The Magician's Nephew*, Digory and Polly observe the evil effects of Jadis's anger.

In *The Horse and His Boy*, Bree, Aravis and Rabadash exhibit pride.

Prince Caspian, says King, shows the sinfulness of the Telmarine monarch Miraz's lust for 'power, wealth and position'.

Each of the seven deadly sins is said to have a 'contrary virtue'. Those virtues are humility, generosity, chastity, charity, moderation, meekness and zeal.

Eustace is greedy in *The Voyage of the 'Dawn Treader'*, and pays the price by turning into a dragon.

The Last Battle, according to King's scheme, is a cautionary tale about envy. Trouble arises when Shift tries to take Aslan's place.

And that leaves us with *The Silver Chair*, and Jill, and the last of the deadly sins, sloth. King defines sloth as 'a disgust with the spiritual because of the physical effort involved'. In Jill's case, he says, it is 'a gradual wearing away of devotion'.

However, as King admits, Jill's forgetfulness begins almost immediately. In my opinion, the forgetfulness doesn't ring true.

Lewis is often criticized for writing about female characters who are dim or who lack willpower and deserve to be punished. The critics may be right to include Jill among the examples. Or it's possible that Lewis simply was rushing his story. Making a character forget something gradually is hard to do in any case. And in fairness to Lewis, when we meet an older Jill in *The Last Battle* she is less of a bumbler. Lewis admirer Paul F. Ford says this new Jill 'reveals a Lewis trying very hard to overcome his sexist outlook' (*Companion to Narnia*).

There were several different lists of serious sins. The seven deadly sins commonly mentioned today primarily come from a list created by St Gregory I (540–604), a pope. Sloth wasn't on Gregory's list. In its place was a sin known by a Greek name, 'accidie', which refers to sadness or a paralysing despair.

WHY DOES PRINCE RILIAN WEAR A MASK?

When Jill meets Prince Rilian, she notices he 'altogether looked a little bit like Hamlet' (*The Silver Chair*, ch.10). Lewis was fascinated by this Shakespearean play. After one rereading he told a friend, 'I am more delighted than ever with the mere atmosphere of it – an atmosphere hard to describe and made up equally of the prevalent sense of death, solitude, & horror and of the extraordinary graciousness and lovableness of H. himself' (*The Collected Letters of C. S. Lewis, Volume 1*, p.91). The atmosphere of *The Silver Chair* is meant to mimic the play.

But Rilian is only Hamlet when he's within the Green Witch's underground castle. That's where the horrors take place. In public, he's someone else: an anonymous knight, face hidden by the visor of his helmet. Those two aspects of Rilian are two sides of Lewis.

For more than thirty years, Lewis lived

Hamlet had been a favourite of Lewis for a long time. He refers to it as the best of Shakespeare's plays in his first notebook for the *Boxen* stories, written when he was about eight years old.

Like most British
soldiers, Lewis
and Paddy
fought in
France. Lewis
was wounded
by shrapnel
from a
misdirected
English shell.
Pieces hit him in
the face, leg
and hand; and a
piece that hit
his side entered
his lung. He had
some shrapnel
in his body for
the rest of his
life, but on the
whole he was
lucky. His
wounds were
the sort that
healed easily in
time. A comrade
standing next to
him was killed.

with Janie Moore (1872–1951), who had been the mother of a friend. Lewis met her when he and the friend, Paddy Moore, were roommates as teenagers in Oxford in 1917. Lewis was eighteen years old. Mrs Moore, forty-five, became something of a replacement mother for Lewis, who referred to her as 'my mother' for many years. She also became his lover. (Mrs Moore had long been separated, though not divorced, from her husband.) In 1918 Paddy Moore was killed in the First World War. Lewis was wounded around the same time, and when he returned to Britain it was Mrs Moore who cared for him.

Mrs Moore could be very generous – in fact her generosity planted the seed of the *Chronicles* in Lewis's imagination. She was the one who invited some convent girls to stay with her and Lewis during the Second World War, which first gave Lewis the idea of a story about some children having an adventure while waiting out the war in the home of an old professor who happened to have a magical wardrobe.

However, their relationship wasn't easy. Mrs Moore dominated Lewis in innumerable ways. She treated him like a servant by inventing petty demands. 'He's as good as an extra maid,' she once said. She lied to him often.

And she never gave up her atheism.

Lewis suffered these slings and arrows silently. So silently, in fact, that the exact nature of the relationship wasn't clear even to Lewis's brother, who lived with them for many years. (They may not have been lovers after Lewis became a Christian in 1931, when he was thirty-two and Mrs Moore was fifty-nine.) A general sense of unease was apparent, but Lewis kept the details to himself. He'd made his choice, he once said. He had no regrets. And though Lewis was figuratively as bound to her as Rilian is to the Green Witch, it seems he found some pleasure in the pain itself.

The relationship became especially bad during Mrs Moore's last years, when her health was not good. Everyone who observed the relationship saw that Lewis was gracious despite the difficulties.

A few months after Mrs Moore entered a nursing home in the spring of 1950, aged seventy-eight, Lewis began writing *The Silver Chair*, in which a demonic witch dominates a young prince. The prince is forced to wear a mask in public. At night, the witch binds the prince to a chair in a room where he can scream without being heard. And when he's finally freed from her spell, she reveals her true serpent form, and he slays her.

In keeping with his relationship with Mrs Moore, Lewis also helped support and even tutor her daughter Maureen, who was only a few years younger than Lewis.

It's completely natural that Lewis would have been angry with Mrs Moore, despite his genuine affection and concern for her. It's just as natural that his feelings would make their way into his novels.

THE LAST BATTLE:
LEWIS'S THOUGHTS

Where's Aslan? Why doesn't he rescue Narnia from its greatest threat? Jewel the unicorn is good enough when it comes to moral philosophy, but he's not a god.

Still, if Aslan has to be kept offstage until the final act, Jewel isn't a bad understudy. The unicorn is a traditional symbol of Christ. In English translations of the Bible it's mentioned several times. (Mistranslations, actually. The original words referred to oxen or horned gazelles, not magical beasts, says translator Gili Bar-Hillel. But the image has stuck.) They appear in art and literature to signify divine innocence and purity. People once believed that unicorn horns had divine healing power.

Shortly before starting the *Chronicles*, Lewis published a poem about a unicorn. '*The Sailing of the Ark*' (later revised and retitled '*The Late Passenger*') describes Noah's sons ignoring 'some animal' who has arrived after

The Last Battle was the second-to-last book Lewis wrote about Narnia. The Magician's Nephew, about Narnia's origins, was finished the next year.

rain has started to fall heavily. Noah's sons ignore the knocking. One complains that it would be too much trouble to make room for one more. Noah wakes up and sees that the animal, who has given up and is leaving in the thick rain, is the unicorn. He's distraught. By turning away the unicorn, he says, his sons have cursed humankind.

The villain of *The Last Battle*, as usual for Lewis, is both dangerous and ridiculous. Lewis referred to Shift the Ape as the 'Antichrist' – the villain in the Bible who convinces people that Jesus is not the saviour. There are scholars who refer to the Antichrist as a demon himself, sometimes even Satan. Lewis didn't give Shift that much credit. As an ape, he's meant to symbolize humankind.

Shift isn't a match for Aslan, but to be consistent with theology Lewis has to keep Aslan hidden. Aslan's appearance has to be a Second Coming, like the anticipated return of Christ to earth, when everyone will be judged. Some of the final judgements Lewis makes spark debates among fans. Should Emeth be saved? Why is there a final twist to the story of the Pevensies? Did Lewis's feelings towards Susan change suddenly? The answers aren't always consistent with the Bible, but they're consistent with Lewis's philosophy.

WHAT IS TASH — AND WHAT ISN'T HE?

LB: Tash

Not every ugly duckling grows up to be a swan. With his demonic bird head, extra arms to grab and claws to rip, he's the sort of demon only a mother could love. To oppose Aslan, Lewis has created a monster that appears to be from a time before Christianity and a place where Christianity never took hold. He reminds Rilian of an idol – a gold-covered stone idol with 'solid diamonds for eyes' (*The Last Battle*, ch.8). He brings to mind Egyptian and Babylonian gods. As a result, reviewers of *The Last Battle* often disagree about what Tash is – idol, god, demon or Satan himself, merely disguised as the chief god in the Calormene pantheon.

This last explanation makes the most sense, given Lewis's feelings. To Lewis, Satan was a very real creature. As Lewis scholar Perry Bramlett puts it, 'Lewis believed that Satan, who represents all the fallen angels, is the

The name Tash is from an old word meaning 'spot' or 'blot' that came to mean a moral fault or stain, even a disgrace or stigma.

It's still used by painters to mean a spot of colour.

power behind death, disease, and sin.' More than that, Lewis says, 'There is no neutral ground in the universe: every square inch, every split second, is claimed by God and counterclaimed by Satan' (*Christian Reflections*, p.33). He wasn't speaking about symbols of good and evil. This wasn't abstract moral philosophy for him. He believed true Christians must accept the existence of Satan as fact.

When Aslan says he and Tash 'are opposites' (*The Last Battle*, ch.15), Lewis isn't implying that they're equal. That's close to a view of good and evil called dualism, which Lewis was careful to reject. In dualism, good and evil are independent of each other. They battle each other as balanced forces. There are dualistic religions – for example, Zoroastrianism, which is older than Christianity and still practised today.

Lewis wrote science fiction novels like *Out of the Silent Planet* (1938) so he could show Satan's influence far beyond Earth.

Lewis didn't believe Satan is God's equal. To him, Satan is one of the angels created by God, and therefore less than God. In Lewis's view, Satan's great fault is to believe himself God's equal. He can't create, as God can. He can only destroy. In Narnia, Aslan creates; Tash is the destroyer. Tash is the form Satan has taken at that time and that place. After all, this is the *last* battle. Lewis wasn't keeping Satan in reserve.

SHOULD ASLAN SAVE EMETH?

When Aslan lets Emeth into heaven at the end of *The Last Battle*, it seems perfectly natural. It fits with both the plot and Aslan's character. Yet the happy ending for Emeth seems to be cause for debate among both casual readers and scholars. Some think Emeth doesn't belong there. More than a few think Lewis was dangerously close to bad ideas. As Emeth's fate reveals, Lewis appears to disagree with central beliefs of his own religion.

Lewis borrowed Emeth's name from Hebrew. It means 'faithful' or 'true'.

SAVINGS ACCOUNTS

In simplest terms, what divides the scholars is the difference between words and deeds. A fundamental rule of Protestant Christianity – Lewis was a Protestant – says a person can reach heaven only by accepting Christ as a saviour. No other figure will do. You can't have faith in something or someone who is merely like Christ, or a symbol for Christ. And it will

A common
interpretation
of Aslan's gift
to Emeth is
that Lewis
believed in
'universalism',
the idea that in
time God will
allow everyone
into heaven, and
even reconcile
with Satan.
There are
branches of
Christianity that
believe this –
though there are
also people who
believe
universalists
aren't Christian,
regardless of
what they call
themselves.
Lewis was
definitely not a
universalist.

not help to live as Christ taught but still not believe that Christ is God's son and that he died and was reborn. In fact, if you have faith, the way you live might not matter, because your sins can be forgiven.

By the strict rules of Protestantism, Emeth should not have been saved. He doesn't believe in Aslan.

As well, one of the defining differences between Protestantism and Catholicism is the question of whether faith alone can save a soul. In Catholicism, salvation comes only when faith is combined with good works. But despite believing in Tash, Emeth is allowed into heaven because of good works: he kept an oath.

This bothers some readers, who feel it's inconsistent with Lewis's Protestant theology. But Lewis's theology was never entirely consistent with Protestantism. In the *Chronicles*, the many examples of Lewis's inconsistencies begin with the very first inhabitant of Narnia, the pagan Mr Tumnus.

It was no different with Emeth. Lewis believed the world was full of people who 'belong to Christ without knowing it'. Perhaps they had heard a different name for Christ, and worshipped him by it. Maybe they'd never had the chance. 'We do not know that only those who know Him can be saved through Him,' Lewis said. He went so far as to include the possibility that some people today are 'led by God's secret influence to concentrate on those parts of their religion which are in agreement with Christianity' (*Mere Christianity*, p.162).

This is different from believing that all religions are the same in essence, and that devotion to an idea of God is what counts. Lewis didn't believe that for a moment. He believed the only saviour is Christ. However, he quoted Christ to explain Emeth:

> And other sheep I have, which are not of this fold: them also I must bring, and they shall hear my voice; and there shall be one fold, and one shepherd. (John 10:16)

Lewis is talking about individuals, of course – the 'secret' Christians within other religions. Still, this is a generous sentiment given Lewis's belief that many other religions are false or even absurd. If the salvation of Emeth doesn't quite fit strict Protestant theology, at least it makes the important point that the Bible allows for some surprises. The lesson may be

Jesus is sometimes called the Good Shepherd because of the same Bible parable Lewis uses to explain Emeth. 'I am the good shepherd: the good shepherd giveth his life for the sheep' (John 10:14).

that it's a mistake to presume to know who will be saved. Lewis himself didn't always live up to that creed, but he knew it was a worthwhile ideal.

WHAT DOES LEWIS MEAN BY 'SHADOWLANDS'?

The Pevensies are a little upset when Narnia is destroyed. Understandably. Lord Digory tries to comfort them by explaining that the Narnia they know is 'a shadow or copy of the real Narnia', which will last forever. Ever the professor, he says, 'It's all in Plato, all in Plato: bless me, what do they teach them at these schools!' (*The Last Battle*, ch.15). Fair enough. Plato's ideas about shadows have been taught for thousands of years. Here's what Lord Digory thought the children should know.

The word 'shadowlands' appears in the *Chronicles* only once, but it's a well-known connection to Lewis because of the film of that name, which tells the story of Lewis's friendship with and marriage to Joy Davidman.

ME AND MY SHADOW

Plato believed there's an ideal world beyond the world we see. What we see, hear, taste, touch and smell are, to use his word, only shadows. We sense only a rough shape of the ideal world and the things in it, the way a shadow is just a rough outline of the object casting it.

169

Plato was born in Athens, sometime around 429 BC. He was a student of Socrates, another great philosopher. Unfortunately, Socrates, who had become involved in politics, angered the rulers of Athens, and was forced to poison himself. Plato, nearly thirty years old, thought it best to leave Athens. He travelled and studied abroad before returning to Athens to found a school, the Academy.

Plato's philosophy was more than just a neat way for Lewis to wrap up the *Chronicles*. Plato is there at the beginning as well. In *The Lion, the Witch and the Wardrobe*, the idea of Deep Magic – natural law in our world – brings Plato into the story. Plato's discussion about shadows is a statement about how to find ideals of right and wrong to follow. He believed we couldn't look only in our own world for those ideals, because what's in our world is always imperfect. He believed we have to keep trying to look beyond the shadows to the true forms, which are universal and timeless.

THE SECOND GOING

Plato's ideal world has been called a Platonic heaven. After death, he believed, our souls are reunited with the true forms. That's what happens to the children in Narnia.

After learning Narnia is going to end, they receive a second shock – they're all dead, along with the Pevensies' parents. But as a reward for keeping their eyes fixed on the Platonic ideal, they can leave the 'Shadowlands', the false England they only thought was real. They get to join Aslan in heaven. He takes them from the shadowlands into the light.

This sudden ending – a train crash that

Aslan reveals with just a paragraph to go before the end of seven volumes – doesn't satisfy every reader. It has even been called cruel. But could Lewis have written any other ending? For him, heaven was where he would see his own mother. In fiction he could arrange what he might have considered a happy accident to see her sooner. Still, making young readers feel the sudden loss of a parent and their own death as well is a hard way to teach the lesson of Christianity's joy. Not everyone shares the fascination with death that Lewis often expressed. The objections are reasonable, whatever the explanation.

LAZY SUSAN

Readers also ask why Susan can't join the others in Narnia. They should take the explanation Lewis offers at face value. She has lost interest in Narnia. She's no longer devoted to its memory.

The real question is, why can't Susan join the others anyway? Is a temporary lack of devotion reason enough for her to miss the train wreck of glory?

Lewis himself lost faith, or seemed to. His own experience must have told him that faith may only seem to disappear before returning stronger than ever.

In 'The Golden Key', a story by one of Lewis's favourite writers, George MacDonald, two children look for 'the way up to the country from which the shadows fall' – heaven. They enter it by opening a door with a golden key found 'at the end of a rainbow'. The key is meant as a symbol of Christ. Paul F. Ford notes that in a personal allusion for Lewis, Peter Pevensie opens the stable door with a golden key.

If it's true that Susan is 'a jolly sight too keen on being grown-up', what's the harm? Aslan has told Lucy, 'every year you grow, you will find me bigger' (*Prince Caspian*, p.10).

A lot has been made about Susan's specific preoccupations. They're the stuff of love. That sort of interest made Lewis uncomfortable in any circumstance – more so when a woman expressed it. All Susan has is a completely natural teenage preoccupation with 'nylons and lipstick and invitations' (*The Last Battle*, ch.12). There's something to the idea that Lewis was punishing Susan for her sexuality, or simply for growing up.

But if you look at the pattern set in the other books, someone was going to have to be punished. Whether the reason Lewis gave was lust or sloth or gluttony or any other sin may not be the point. The ending would have been more of a surprise if Aslan hadn't found fault with one of the Pevensies.

Lewis believed in judgement and in the Judgement Day. He believed the Second Coming was going to happen. And, he said, 'precisely because we cannot predict the moment, we must be ready at all moments' (*The World's Last Night,* p.107). We can't wait to make choices about God until the moment comes, he said. By then it will be too late.

Poor Susan: a victim of bad timing. She might have become just as devoted as Lewis eventually became – maybe even at a younger age than when Lewis became religious again. But she wasn't ready when the moment came.

Or perhaps she'll have a second chance. Though people may have died in the train wreck, and Narnia may have seen its Second Coming, our world is still puttering along at the end of *The Last Battle*. She may yet join her family in heaven.

In an odd way, she could turn out to be more like Lewis than any of the other characters. She's about to learn that her whole family has died and that she's alone in the world – much like Lewis felt after his mother died. It took a long time for those events to lead him to the Aslan of our world, but it happened. The same could be true for Susan. Given that Aslan has growled, snarled, clawed, chased and scolded the other children on their path to heaven, the train wreck that killed everyone she loved most may be another reminder from Aslan to love him most of all.

Author Neil Gaiman has written a fascinating short story, 'The Problem of Susan', inside the mind of Susan as an adult. (It can be found in *Flights: Extreme Visions Of Fantasy*, edited by Al Sarrantonio and published by Roc/Penguin.)

AFTERWORD:
WHY WOULD ANYONE
HATE NARNIA?

Since you're reading this book, you're almost certainly a fan of the *Chronicles*. Are you surprised to learn many people hate them?

The critics say the real Lewis behind the public persona wasn't as generous with his Christian love as he appeared. They claim he was often cruelly racist and sexist, and that this is reflected in the *Chronicles*.

It can be difficult to find people on either side of the debate who are willing to approach it with an open mind. Perhaps that's to be expected when the subjects are religion and race and gender. What's more personal?

It's worth considering the questions raised by the critics. Lewis meant Narnia as more than entertainment. He wanted young readers to develop what are called 'stock responses' – an idea that goes back to Plato, and which Lewis himself defines perfectly: 'The little human animal will not at first have the right responses. It must be trained to feel pleasure, liking, disgust and hatred at those things which are really pleasant, likeable, disgusting and hateful' (*The Abolition of Man*, p.14).

How might the little human animal be affected if Lewis

himself was strongly racist or sexist? Are those characteristics in Narnia? Did Lewis mean to pass them on to readers, or were they unconscious and unavoidable reflections of the attitudes of his time? And what about Lewis's religious views? He's often considered a broad-minded Christian, emphasizing beliefs common to most of the different branches of Christianity. Is that accurate? Is that what's in Narnia?

Sadly, the evidence is unsettling. Lewis was capable of admirable generosity in his personal life and his ideas. But he could be thoroughly obnoxious about people who thought differently from him or even those who looked different. For example, to him Chinese were 'Chinks', and were 'human (or roughly human) in form but in nothing else'. When his brother Warren, visiting China, complained in a letter that 'it is impossible to visualize these disgusting creatures as human beings at all or even as animals', Lewis expressed agreement in terms you'd hardly expect from the creator of Narnia: 'One can't help feeling that when people are so very different as all that, one has no business to be connected with them at all' (*The Collected Letters of C. S. Lewis, Volume 1*, p.711).

I'd like to think that even Lewis's strongest defenders wouldn't try to defend that belief or others like it that Lewis expressed. And it can't be hard to understand why the objects of Lewis's disgust might be wary of the ideas he hoped to train.

An unpleasant possibility must be considered: some people hate Narnia because the creator of Narnia hated them. 'Hate' is a strong word, but it was Lewis's, and he used it emphatically. '[A] hardened bigot shouting every one down till he had no friends left is what I am in danger of becoming,' he wrote to a friend when he was in his thirties. 'You have no idea how much of my time I spend just *hating* people whom I disagree with – tho' I know them only from their books – and inventing conversations in which I score off them.' (*The Collected Letters of C. S. Lewis, Volume 2*, p.125–6).

Lewis biographer Humphrey Carpenter, who knew Lewis and whose father, the Anglican Bishop of Oxford, was asked to perform Lewis's marriage, describes the serious personality flaw behind the problem: 'There is often an unnecessarily bullying weight to his arguments, particularly if he is putting down an opponent. When he disagrees with a remark he tends to tear it from its context and wave it at the reader, blinded by his feelings from considering the real meaning of the writer . . . Such a manner of dealing with a subject grew largely from Lewis's susceptibility to prejudices . . .' (*The Inklings*, p.222). (Carpenter means prejudices in general, not specifically ethnic bigotry as the word is often used. Lewis's prejudices were as strong in literary matters or politics.)

Lewis's admission 'tho' I know them only from their books' points to another interesting fact. His opinions were second-hand. Warren had been to China, and to Africa as well. Lewis, except for war service in France and a short trip to Greece at the end of his life, never left Britain. It's hard not to think of Mark Twain's maxim 'Travel is fatal to prejudice, bigotry, and narrow-mindedness.'

Lewis's prejudices were hardly limited to Asians. Lewis viewed many other ethnicities as only roughly human in form. He also viewed other religions, including branches of Christianity, as only roughly religious, or not religious at all.

Lewis understood, as he wrote in books intended for the public, that racism is vile and has no place in the heart of a Christian. But both his private correspondence and his books are spiced with bigotry that is anything but unconscious, and is often dressed up as a theory. With little or no serious experience of his own, he was happy to parrot racist comments he heard or read. Muslims lie; Jews are greedy; Africans are sex-crazed; Italians are bombastic. These kinds of remarks are different from a thoughtful rejection of, say, Islam or Judaism. They're a conscious acceptance of the nonsense he heard from others. It's impossible to reconcile this part of Lewis's personality with the part that wanted to be intellectually sound in all of his beliefs. His remarks were too frequent to be dismissed as misunderstood or a minor aspect of the man.

Lewis can't be judged harshly for believing in his religion and disbelieving others. Of course he didn't rate Islam or Hinduism or Judaism as highly as Christianity. He thought they were essentially wrong. However, judged even by the standards he set for himself, Lewis's attitude towards other religions is surprisingly bigoted. He wanted very much to use intellectual arguments to prove Christianity more valid than other religions, and he wanted to find a common ground among Christians. He had great difficulty doing either. He didn't merely argue that other religions were wrong; he tried to argue them out of existence. Hinduism, he believed, isn't a real religion because it doesn't deny anything. Truth can't exist where nothing is false. (A neat theory, but it doesn't have a lot to do with Hinduism.) Everything other than Hinduism is worse – just a minor, erroneous and inferior version of

Hinduism or Christianity that no 'adult mind' would choose. Lewis's favourite argumentative trick was to take two wholly unrelated religions and say one was 'nothing more' than the other. Islam is nothing more than 'polygamous Methodism'; Judaism is nothing more than the beliefs of Plymouth Brethren. (Plymouth Brothers avoid ritual and clergy, which makes their religion light years from Judaism.) This is the sort of intellectually unsound argument that Humphrey Carpenter mentioned. In trying to make different beliefs look absurd, Lewis makes himself look foolish. All because he couldn't get past his prejudices.

What makes his habit harder to understand is that he was furious when the same kind of argument was used against Christianity. He 'abhorred' the sort of person who did this, says Lewis scholar Paul F. Ford. 'Such persons are always given away by their use of the words "nothing but", "merely", or "only"' (*Companion to Narnia*, p.345). In Narnia, as Ford points out, Lewis ridicules people who use that approach to argue away Christianity. In *The Silver Chair*, when the Green Witch refers to Aslan as nothing but a big cat and the sun nothing but a lamp, she's meant to look foolish. To even casual observers of the religions against which Lewis argued, and certainly to the scholars of those religions, Lewis comes across as the Green Witch does. There's no good explanation for Lewis's double standards.

Like his feelings about other races, Lewis's feelings about other Christian sects were often bigotry rather than the product of scholarship. There's a revealing story about his *Mere Christianity*, a collection of essays that he hoped would express 'the common doctrines of Christianity' (*Mere Christianity*, p.xii) to the general public. (It began as a series of radio broadcasts for the BBC.) Because of the theme, Lewis sent draft scripts to four clergymen friends – an Anglican, a Presbyterian, a Methodist and a Roman Catholic. (No, this is not the beginning of a joke.) The Methodist and the Roman Catholic were 'hostile' in their response. Lewis had failed to overcome his bias even when the point of the exercise was diplomacy. Regarding Catholicism, Lewis admitted, 'At my first coming into the world I had been (implicitly) warned never to trust a Papist' (*Surprised by Joy*, p.216). He believed he overcame this feeling when he became close to J. R. R. Tolkien. But Tolkien, who loved Lewis dearly, didn't agree. As Tolkien remarked, when rumours of atrocities against priests and nuns in Spain during the 1930s reached the news, 'If a Lutheran is put in jail he [Lewis] is up in arms; but if Catholics are slaughtered – he disbelieves it, and I daresay really thinks they ask for it. There is a good deal of Ulster [a Protestant stronghold of Ireland] still left in C. S. L, if hidden from himself' (Humphrey Carpenter, *The Inklings*, p.192).

Branches of Protestantism didn't fare any better. If anything, some annoyed Lewis more. He attacked Quakers often and believed 'it seems more useful not to classify them as Christians' (*Letters of C. S. Lewis*, p.482). He made similar remarks about other sects. The comments show Lewis was often inclined to find differences than shared ideals.

When Lewis saw this side of himself, he didn't like it. After the death of Arthur Greeves, the friend to whom he had admitted his passionate bigotry in the letter quoted earlier, he compared himself to Greeves. The quality in his friend that made the deepest impression was 'charity', which Lewis noted was the opposite of his own 'arrogance'. Lewis suggested his friend be remembered this way: 'He *despised* nothing.' What Lewis admired most was his friend's lack of a quality that Lewis disliked in himself. 'Contempt – if not the worst, surely the most ludicrously inappropriate of the sins . . .' Lewis added that Greeves '. . .fulfilled the Gospel precept: he "judged not"' (*The Collected Letters of C. S. Lewis, Volume 1,* p.995).

And what about women? Lewis was a harsh judge. If he thought a woman was ugly, he belittled her; if he thought she was beautiful, he feared her power over him. Both of those views are in Narnia. At the end of *The Last Battle*, Susan Pevensie is no longer a friend of Narnia because she has discovered lipstick and nylons. She's punished for her sexual feelings – and for Lewis's. In *Prince Caspian*, some of the schoolchildren are 'dumpy, prim little girls with fat legs' (*Prince Caspian*, ch.14). Literary critic John Goldthwaite, who believes 'Lewis's hatreds were petty, his enemies weak', makes a good point: '[S]omewhere among the world's vast population of dumpy people with fat legs, there is one crestfallen schoolgirl who understands all too well the message of saintly [Lewis] in this passage.' Goldthwaite sums up Lewis's attitudes towards all the girls of the *Chronicles*: 'If they must tag along, that is, they had better follow orders, show pluck, and not blubber over all those things they can usually be expected to blubber over. Most will be found wanting along the way, naturally, and the reasons will be tediously familiar: "She's not like Lucy, you know, who's as good as a man, or at any rate as good as a boy'" (*The Natural History of Make-Believe*, p.228).

Another serious example of Lewis's bigotry in the *Chronicles* are the Calormenes. Many critics have noted the Calormenes are described with a catalogue of racist remarks about Muslims. Calormenes would sooner lie than tell the truth; they can't think logically; they're cruel to animals, and crueller to people; they're filthy; they worship idols. In *Companion to Narnia*, Paul F. Ford dutifully presents these details and then, after four pages, adds a footnote: 'Like many Englishmen of his era, Lewis was unconsciously unsympathetic to things and people Middle-Eastern. That Lewis opts into this cultural blindness is regrettable' (*Companion to Narnia*, p.95). But there was nothing unconscious about these feelings, as his letters prove. It's as if instead of cribbing from E. Nesbit as he did for his plots, Lewis wrote about the Calormenes while reading the memoirs of the British colonial ruler, Lord Cromer. About 'Orientals' – the name once used to slur all Eastern and Middle Eastern peoples at the same time – Cromer warned: 'Want of accuracy, which easily degenerates into untruthfulness, is in fact the main characteristic of the Oriental mind. The European is a close reasoner; his statements of fact are devoid of any ambiguity; he is a natural logician . . . The mind of the Oriental, on the other hand, like his picturesque streets, is eminently wanting in symmetry. His reasoning is of the most slipshod description' (*Modern Egypt*, p.168). Wandering streets in Cairo reveal a wandering 'Oriental' mind? Cromer had been away from London too long, as any tourist without a street map knows. Lewis repeats the nonsense.

The Calormenes are not just funny villains in a story that

everyone would agree needs villains of one sort or another. Lewis was very conscious of using them as learning tools. Lewis scholar and admirer Doris Myers, analysing *The Horse and His Boy* in terms of stock responses intended by Lewis, concludes that 'All the senses are engaged to influence the reader to hate Calormen and love Narnia.' Lewis scholar Peter Schakel admits, 'One may well regret the emphasis on the dark skins and the garlicky breath of the Calormenes and the dwarf's references to the Calormenes as "darkies"' (*Reading With the Heart*, p.13). Yes, one may. The emphasis is hateful and ignorant, as is the word. But he and Doris Myers believe readers who find racism are not reading properly. They say Lewis is merely repeating motifs found in medieval poetry. They're wrong to reduce it or intellectualize it. For Lewis, bad feelings between Christianity and Islam weren't confined to the past. They were part of national life. In Lewis's lifetime, Britain jockeyed with the Islamic Ottoman Empire, then fought against Turkey in the First World War. In that conflict Britain gained control of a large part of the Middle East, where it established colonial rule. (British didn't cede the Suez Canal to Egypt until 1956, after the Chronicles were written. Even then Britain almost went to war to keep it.) Also, Lewis didn't object only to the religious tenets of Islam. He ridiculed non-religious aspects of Islamic people. That sort of racism sold a lot of newspapers and books during Lewis's lifetime. It wasn't confined to the medieval poetry. Even if it had been, that would make no difference. The fact that a racist belief is old doesn't make it less racist. Lewis knew that the themes in medieval poetry originated in real hatred. Calling the racism a 'motif' and saying it comes from literature doesn't make it better than if Lewis had based his characters on a dusty book of racist jokes.

Nor is it an argument against Lewis's racism when the Calormene soldier Emeth is allowed into heaven in *The Last Battle*. It's the exception that proves the rule. Throughout Lewis's life, he held bigoted views of certain people as a class despite liking individuals from that group. Far from being evidence that he was open-minded, it shows that he ignored the evidence in front him. He viewed his friends as exceptional cases. It's often mentioned that the woman he married towards the end of life, Joy Davidman, was Jewish, and that Lewis must have been open-minded about Judaism for him to marry her. That's not accurate. Her parents were atheists and raised her as one. Lewis explained her true feelings to a friend: she believed 'the only living Judaism is Christianity', and 'where her own people still have any religion it is archaic, pedantic . . .' (*Reflections on the Psalms*, p.76). Joy Davidman wasn't an example of Lewis's open mind; she was the authority he cited for racist views he'd held since he was a child. In his *Boxen* stories he created animals that were, in his own words, stand-ins for Jews. He described them as 'an abomination, as a class'. Of course, he was precocious enough to have also absorbed at that early age an adult justification for racism: the hero of his story 'was sensible enough not to condemn' an individual he liked, even if that individual was from a class that was an abomination (*Boxen*, p.100). Lewis found no problem with these comments when he reread them as an adult.

Can Lewis be blamed for failing to outgrow what he would

have called the stock responses of his childhood training? Perhaps not. Lessons taught that early are hard to outgrow. His supporters defend him with that truth. His critics wonder what it means for the lessons the *Chronicles* are meant to teach.

The best we can do is judge Lewis on his terms. That doesn't mean judging him by the morality of his time, as some apologists have done. Lewis hated that sort of thing. He didn't like it when people of his time treated the past as a period of cultural or moral infancy, and we do him no service by making the same mistake in his case. He would not have appreciated being treated as feeble. It would also be inaccurate. He made clear in his writing that he knew racism was wrong. He simply failed to live up to those statements. He didn't condemn sexism as he did racism, but he was certainly aware of it as an issue. He also knew that even in his time his belief in the intellectual inferiority of women was noticed. Self-awareness wasn't strong enough to break him from his prejudices.

Even more important, Lewis didn't believe morality changes from year to year. Lewis believed in natural law, 'Moral Law' as he sometimes called it, the unchanging sense of right and wrong that he believed God put in all of us. Lewis once said, 'There is nothing indulgent about the Moral Law. It is as hard as nails. It tells you to do the straight thing and it does not seem to care how painful, or dangerous, or difficult it is to do so' (*Mere Christianity*, p.37).

And how does Lewis fare by that immortal code? Though it may be difficult for some Narnia fans to admit, he does not fare well.

There's a reason why admirers feel obliged to make apologies and offer explanations. It's the same reason a committed Christian wrote in *The Atlantic* a few years ago: 'Even as a fan I must admit that certain passages made me wince. For example, the wicked dwarfs ridicule the Calormenes as "darkies"; I skirted the word, because I don't want it in my kids' heads'. That same commentator also 'reworded' the passage about Susan not getting to heaven, because Lewis 'seems to have held his character's sexual independence against her' (Gregg Easterbrook, *In Defense of C. S. Lewis*).

Lewis himself could tell you that's Moral Law at work. He knew that theories about medieval literary motifs mean nothing when you have a feeling in the pit of your stomach that a word or an image is wrong and cruel and not something you want your children to learn.

It's simply not enough to say Lewis made exceptions for people he knew. If you find that difficult to believe, test your own gut: invite a black friend or a Muslim friend or a Chinese friend over to dinner at your home and tell them you believe the awful things people say about their race or religion. Repeat a few of them – better yet, read some of the things Lewis wrote about them. Then explain that you like them anyway because they're not like all the rest.

A nauseating thought, isn't it? That's Moral Law at work. You can't do it because you know it's wrong.

You can forgive Lewis if you like. That might be consistent with the *Chronicles*. But the next time someone says they hate Lewis or hate Narnia, take a moment to ask if they feel Lewis hated them first.

BIBLIOGRAPHY AND SUGGESTIONS
FOR FURTHER READING

Some books have been especially helpful in researching this one, and readers who are interested in Lewis should look for them. Paul F. Ford's *Companion to Narnia*, which I've cited often, is a superb reference. It's primarily an encyclopedia of people, places and things in the *Chronicles*. For example, it gathers the various facts about Aslan that are spread over all the books and presents them in one entry. More interesting, in my opinion, are the comments and historical references Ford adds in his occasional foot notes. Also, even the most expert Lewis scholars are indebted to Ford's work in finding allusions to the Bible. He's the authority on whom everyone relies. For a broader look at Lewis's work and life, it's worth finding *The C. S. Lewis Reader's Encyclopedia*, edited by Jeffrey D. Schultz and John G. West Jr. More than forty Lewis scholars contributed to it. The personalities of some of the contributors come though in their entries, which adds to the interest of the book. Walter Hooper's *C. S. Lewis: A Companion and Guide* was also helpful and might interest some Lewis researchers. Much longer than the *Reader's Encyclopedia*, and not as easy for a casual reader to navigate, it reflects Hooper's detailed knowledge of Lewis and his professional connections to Lewis's literary estate. Hooper's biography, written with Roger Lancelyn Green, is an enjoyable read, though not objective enough to be the final word. Some scholars think A. N. Wilson's biography is controversial – maybe even scandalous – but in fact it's thoughtful and packed with observations that you won't find elsewhere. Because Lewis was so prolific, Janine Goffar has done a real service by compiling the *C. S. Lewis Index*, which collects key thoughts from his works and arranges them by subject. *Reading the Classics with C. S. Lewis*, a collection of essays edited by Thomas L. Martin, is also worthwhile.

Finally, if you want to offer further reading to a very young Lewis fan, I'd recommend *The Man Who Created Narnia*, by Michael Coren (Toronto: Lester Publishing, 1994) and *The Land of Narnia: Brian Sibley Explores the World of C. S. Lewis* by Brian Sibley (New York: HarperCollins, 1990). Both are excellent. Coren's book has many photographs. Sibley's book has illustrations by Pauline Baynes, who illustrated the original editions of the *Chronicles*.

BIBLIOGRAPHY

BOOKS

Carpenter, Humphrey. *The Inklings: C. S. Lewis, J. R. R. Tolkien, Charles Williams, and Their Friends* (London: Allen & Unwin, 1978) Copyright © 1978 George Allen & Unwin (Publishers) Ltd, 1978

Coren, Michael. *The Man Who Created Narnia : The Story of C. S. Lewis* (Toronto: Lester, 1994) Copyright © 1994 Michael Coren

Ford, Paul F. *Companion to Narnia* (San Francisco: HarperSanFrancisco, 1994)

Goffar, Janine. *C. S. Lewis Index : Rumours from the Sculptor's Shop* (Carlisle: Solway, 1995) Copyright © 1995 Janine Goffar

Goldthwaite, John. *The Natural History of Make-Believe: A Guide to the Principal Works of Britain, Europe, and America* (New York: Oxford University Press, 1996) Copyright © 1996 John Goldthwaite

Green, Roger Lancelyn and Walter Hooper. *C. S. Lewis: A Biography* rev. ed. (San Diego: Harcourt, 1994) Copyright © 1974 Richard Lancelyn Green, as Literary Executor for the Estate of Roger Lancelyn Green, and Walter Hooper

Hooper, Walter. *C. S. Lewis : A Companion & Guide* (London: HarperCollins, 1996) Copyright © 1996 C. S. Lewis Pte Ltd

Hooper, Walter. *Past Watchful Dragons* (New York: Collier, 1979)

Karkkainen, Paul A. *Narnia Explored* (Old Tappan, NJ: Revell, 1979) Copyright © 1979 Paul A. Karkkainen

Lewis, C.S. *The Abolition of Man* (New York: Macmillan, 1947) Copyright © 1944, 1947, C. S. Lewis Pte Ltd. Copyright renewed © 1971, 1974, C. S. Lewis Pte Ltd

— *Boxen: The Imaginary World of the Young C. S. Lewis* Edited by Walter Hooper (London: Collins, 1985) Copyright © 1985 C. S. Lewis Pte Ltd

— *The Collected Letters of C. S. Lewis, Volume 1* (New York: HarperCollins, 2004) Copyright © 2004 C. S. Lewis Pte Ltd

— *The Collected Letters of C. S. Lewis, Volume 2* (New York: HarperCollins, 2004) Copyright © 2004 C. S. Lewis Pte Ltd

— *The Essential C. S. Lewis* Edited by Lyle W. Dorsett (New York: Macmillan, 1988)

— *God In the Dock: Essays on Theology and Ethics* Edited by Walter Hooper (Grand Rapids: Eerdmans, 1970) Copyright © 1970 Trustees of the Estate of C. S. Lewis

— 'It All Began With a Picture' reprinted in *Of Other Worlds: Essays and Stories*, edited by Walter Hooper (London: G. Bles, 1966) Copyright © 1966 C. S. Lewis Pte Ltd Copyright renewed © 1994 C. S. Lewis Pte Ltd

— *Letters of C. S. Lewis* Copyright © 1966 W.H. Lewis Copyright © 1966, 1988 C. S. Lewis Pte Ltd

— *Letters to Children* Edited by Lyle W. Dorsett and Marjorie Lamp Mead (London: Collins, 1985) Copyright © 1985 C. S. Lewis Pte Ltd

— *Mere Christianity* (New York: Macmillan, 1960) Copyright © 1952, C. S. Lewis Pte Ltd Copyright renewed © 1980 C. S. Lewis Pte Ltd

— *Miracles, a preliminary study* (New York: Macmillan, 1977) Copyright © 1947 C. S. Lewis Pte Ltd Copyright renewed © 1974 C. S. Lewis Pte Ltd Revised 1960, restored 1996 C. S. Lewis Pte Ltd

— *Out of The Silent Planet* (New York: Macmillan, 1949) Copyright © 1938 C. S.

Lewis Pte Ltd
— *Poems* (New York: Harcourt, Brace & World, 1964) Copyright © 1964 C. S. Lewis Pte Ltd Copyright renewed © 1992 by C. S. Lewis Pte Ltd
— *Reflections on the Psalms* (New York: Harcourt, Brace, 1958) Copyright © 1958 C. S. Lewis Pte Ltd. Copyright renewed 1986 Arthur Owen Barfield
— *Spenser's Images of Life* Edited by Alistair Fowler (Cambridge: Cambridge University Press, 1967) Copyright © 1967 Cambridge University Press
— *Surprised by Joy: The Shape of My Early Life* (London: G. Bles, 1955) Copyright © 1955 C. S. Lewis Pte Ltd
— *The Pilgrim's Regress* (Grand Rapids: Eerdmans, 1992) Copyright © 1933, 1943 Clive Staples Lewis
— *The Weight of Glory* (New York: Macmillan, 1980) Copyright © 1949 C. S. Lewis Pte Ltd Copyright renewed © 1976, revised 1980 C. S. Lewis Pte Ltd
— *The World's Last Night and Other Essays* (New York: Harcourt Brace & World, 1960) Copyright © 1960, 1958, 1955 C. S. Lewis Pte Ltd Copyright © 1952 C. S. Lewis Pte Ltd Copyright renewed 1988, 1986 Arthur Owen Barfield; Copyright © 1959 Helen Joy Lewis; Copyright renewed 1987 Arthur Owen Barfield
Martin, Thomas L. (ed.). *Reading the Classics with C. S. Lewis* (Grand Rapids: Baker, 2000) Copyright © 2000 Thomas L. Martin
Myers, Doris T. *C. S. Lewis In Context* (Kent, Ohio: Kent State University Press, 1994) Copyright © 1994 Kent State University Press
Said, Edward W. *Orientalism* (New York: Pantheon, 1978)
Schakel, Peter J. *Reading with the Heart: The Way into Narnia* (Grand Rapids: Eerdmans, 1979) Copyright © 1979 Wm. B. Eerdmans Publishing Co (see www.readingwiththeheart.com)
Schultz, Jeffrey D., and John G. West, Jr. (eds.). *The C. S. Lewis Readers' Encyclopedia* (Grand Rapids: Zondervan, 1998) Copyright © 1998 Jeffrey D. Schultz. & Co
Tolkien, J. R. R. *The Lord of the Rings* (London: HarperCollins, 1994) Copyright © 1954, 1965, 1966 J. R. R. Tolkien; 1954 edition copyright © renewed 1982 Christopher R. Tolkien, Michael H.R. Tolkien, John F. R. Tolkien and Priscilla M. A. R. Tolkien; 1965/1966 editions copyright © renewed 1993, 1994 Christopher R. Tolkien, John F .R. Tolkien and Priscilla M. A. R. Tolkien
Wilson, A. N. *C. S. Lewis: A Biography* (New York: Ballantine, 1990) Copyright © 1990 A.N. Wilson

ARTICLES
Downing, David C. 'The Dungeon of his Soul': Lewis's Unfinished 'Quest of Bleheris'
Easterbrook, Gregg. 'In Defense of C. S. Lewis', *The Atlantic Monthly*, October 2001
King, Don. W. 'Narnia and the Seven Deadly Sins' by Don W. King, first appeared in *Mythlore* 10 (Spring 1984): pp.14–19
Nicholson, Mervyn. 'C. S. Lewis and the Scholarship of the Imagination in E. Nesbit and Rider Haggard', *Renascence*, Fall 98, Vol 51, Issue 1, p.41
Usher, Jonathan. 'A Narnian Odyssey'. *Electronic Bulletin of the Dante Society of America*, 12 March 2001

Introduction:

page 13: 'hidden story': *Letters to Children*, p.III.

page 14: Spenser: *Spenser's Images of Life* (Cambridge: Cambridge University Press, 1967).

page 14: 'picture': from the essay 'It All Began With a Picture', reprinted in *Of Other Worlds: Essays and Stories*, C. S. Lewis; edited by Walter Hooper (London:G. Bles, 1966).

page 14: 'CSL says': *The Afterlife: Essays and Criticism*, Penelope Fitzgerald (New York: Counterpoint, 2003), p.249.

page 15: 'romp': *The Encyclopedia of Fantasy*, John Clute and John Grant (New York: St Martin's, 1999).

page 17: 'nameless longings': Robert Louis Stevenson, 'A Gossip on Romance', *Longman's Magazine*, 1:1 (November 1882), pp.69–79. Reprinted in *Memories and Portraits* (1887), pp.247–74. Possible online resource: http://pages.prodigy.net/rogers99/rls_gossip_on_romance.html

THE LION, THE WITCH AND THE WARDROBE
Introduction:

page 19: Narnia name: *Companion to Narnia*, p.299. Possible online resource: http://www.pford.stjohnsem.edu/ford/cslewis/index.htm

page 19: Dedication to Lucy Barfield: Walter Hooper's *C. S. Lewis: A Companion & Guide* offers extensive material on the dedicatees of all the Narnia books. There's also a chart in *The C. S. Lewis Readers' Encyclopedia.*

page 20: Sir Peter Mouse: *Boxen: The Imaginary World of the Young C. S. Lewis* has historical detail and commentary from Walter Hooper. It also reproduces some of Lewis's drawings.

page 20: Vertumnus: *Companion to Narnia*, p.428. Paul F. Ford cites Lewis scholar Nancy-Lou Patterson as the source for the observation that Tumnus and Vertumnus are connected. If you disapprove of the connection made to Pomona, blame this author, not her.

page 21: Aslan name: *Companion to Narnia*, p.63.

page 23: 'not exactly like': *Letters to Children*, p.93. See also p.52.

Wardrobe:

page 26: Gresham on wardrobe: *Bookpage*, March 1999, interview by Miriam E. Drennan. Possible online resource: http://www.bookpage.com/9903bp/douglas_gresham.html

page 27: 'tradition of E. Nesbit': this is the account of Chad Walsh, an early Lewis scholar, in *C. S. Lewis: Apostle to the Skeptics* (1949), p.10, quoted in *C. S. Lewis: A Companion & Guide*, Hooper, p.402.

page 28: 'They are E. Nesbit children': *C. S. Lewis: A Biography*, A. N. Wilson, p.221.

page 28: **'The extent of Lewis's borrowing'**: Mervyn Nicholson, 'C. S. Lewis and the Scholarship of the Imagination in E Nesbit and Rider Haggard', *Renascence*, Fall 98, Vol 51, Issue 1, p.41.

page 29: **Fabian Society**: for Rowling's use, see *The Magical Worlds of Harry Potter*, David Colbert, rev. ed (2003).

JADIS:

page 32: **Snow Queen**: text from English translation by H. P. Paulli (1872). Possible online resource: http://www.heindorffhus.dk/frame-Andersen19-SnowQueen.htm

page 33: **'The Quest of Belheris'**: David C. Downing, of Elizabethtown College, PA, offers a discussion of this unpublished poem (though without reference to Villon), which he reviewed in manuscript, in 'The Dungeon of his Soul': Lewis's Unfinished 'Quest of Bleheris'. His citation of the original source: 'The Quest of Bleheris.' Manuscript in the Bodleian Library, Oxford (MS. Eng. lett. c. 220/5 fols. 5–43). Copies at the Marion C. Wade Center, Wheaton College. Possible online resource: http://users.etown.edu/d/DOWNINDC/dungeon.htm

page 34: **'Circe' character**: in an unpublished letter quoted in *Reading With the Heart*, Peter Schakel, p.9.

page 38: **'Jadis owes more to Haggard'**: Nicholson, op. cit.

page 39: **Haggard 'could slip'**: Clute and Grant, op. cit.

page 40: **'God then formed Lilith'**: *Hebrew Myths* by Robert Graves and Raphael Patai (New York: Doubleday, 1964), pp.65–69.

page 41: **'[Lilith] refused'**: Schakel, op. cit., pp.139–40.

DEEP MAGIC:

page 43: **'From his first book of prose'**: 'The Natural Law', Kathryn Lindskoog, entry in *The C. S. Lewis Readers' Encyclopedia*, p.290.

ASLAN:

page 48: **World Ash Tree**: Paul F. Ford's *Companion to Narnia* has a full list of changes in the text of various editions.

page 50: **Christ 'did not, as a man'**: Ford, *Companion to Narnia*, p.21.

WHITE STAG:

page 55: **Physiologus**: *Physiologus*, trans. by Alan Wood Rendell (London: Bumpus, 1928). Possible online resource: http://bestiary.ca/etexts/rendell1928/rendell1928.htm

THE MAGICIAN'S NEPHEW

DIGORY KIRKE:

page 62: **Kirkpatrick**: Lewis's memoir *Surprised by Joy* is the likely source for most descriptions of Kirkpatrick. For a different view, look at A. N. Wilson's biography of Lewis. Wilson is not as warm towards Kirkpatrick as Lewis. Even if you disagree with some of his observations, they're worth considering.

page 66: 'disliking the twentieth century': Fitzgerald, op. cit., p.250.

page 66: 'Among the last': *Life Isn't Fair*, Harold Hill (Perigee: New York, 1997).

RINGS:

page 68: 'English binges': Wilson, pp.131–2.

page 68: 'people with vague': *The Inklings*, p.67.

page 69: Edward Tangye Lean: Carpenter, *The Inklings*, p.57.

page 69: *The Lord of The Rings*: 'great power', vol. II, ch.9; 'Orcs reeled', vol. II, ch.7.

page 70: 'One of us should': Duriez, Colin, *Tolkien and C. S. Lewis: The Gift of Friendship*, p.177.

page 75: 'Only from him': *The Inklings*, p.32.

page 76: 'my long night talk': *The Inklings*, p.45.

MRS LEFAY:

page 77: 'Lefay Fragment': The Lefay fragment is printed in full in Walter Hooper's *Past Watchful Dragons: The Narnian Chronicles of C. S. Lewis* (New York: Collier Books, 1979).

HALL OF IMAGES:

page 87: 'The father will not agree': *The Homeric Hymns and Homerica*, Hesiod; trans. by Hugh G. Evelyn-White (Cambridge, MA.:Harvard University Press; London: Heinemann, 1914).

DEPLORABLE WORD:

page 91: Dolorous Stroke: Paul F. Ford, *Companion to Narnia*

page 93: 'charnel': Ford credits Professor T.W. Craik.

page 94: 'keep their true names secret': *The Golden Bough*, Sir James George Frazer (New York: Macmillan, 1922) ch 22. Possible online resource: http://www.bartleby.com/196

page 94: 'Because Adam tried to compel her': *Hebrew Myths*, op. cit.

THE HORSE AND HIS BOY

INTRODUCTION:

page 97: 'emphasis': *Reading with the Heart: The Way into Narnia*, Peter J. Schakel (Grand Rapids: Eerdmans, 1979), p.13. Possible online resource: http://www.hope.edu/academic/english/schakel/readingwiththeheart/

page 97: 'regrettable': *Companion to Narnia*, p.95.

BREE:

page 99: doubting Thomas: The connection to the disciple Thomas, noted by many readers, was probaby first made by Paul F. Ford, as one of the many Bible allusions he has identified.

SHASTA:

page 103: Otto Rank: readers interested in more of Rank's ideas should start with *The Myth of the Birth of the Hero*, available in many editions including a new translation published by John Hopkins University Press in 2004.

KNIGHT:
page 108: **Winter's Tale:** personal correspondence between Joshua Kronengold
and Liz Katz.

NORTHNESS:
page 111: **'I heard a voice':** 'Tegner's Drapa', in *The Seaside and the Fireside*, Henry
Wadsworth Longfellow, 1850.
page 112: **'In the decades before the First World War':** A.N. Wilson, op. cit. p.29.

PRINCE CASPIAN
INTRODUCTION:
page 116: **'Jardis':** *C. S. Lewis: A Biography*, rev. ed, Roger Lancelyn Green and
Walter Hooper (Orlando: Harcourt, 1994), p.250.

FAITH:
page 130: **'What does the effect':** 'Prince Caspian,' Paul F. Ford, entry in
The C. S. Lewis Readers' Encyclopedia, op. cit., p.337.

THE VOYAGE OF THE 'DAWN TREADER'
INTRODUCTION:
page 136: **Dante:** 'A Narnian Odyssey', Jonathan Usher, Electronic Bulletin of the
Dante Society of America, 12 March 2001. Internet resource:
http://www.princeton.edu/~dante/ebdsa/usher032001.htm

DARK ISLAND:
page 141: **Lewis made a revision:** Both Paul F. Ford's *Companion to Narnia* and
Walter Hooper's *C. S. Lewis: A Companion & Guide* provide details
about the differences in various editions.

THE SILVER CHAIR
INTRODUCTION:
page 145: **'drove him into the form':** A. N. Wilson, op.cit., pp.210–15. See also
Hooper, *C. S. Lewis Companion & Guide*, pp.618–19. And 'G. E. M.
Anscombe', Katherine Harper, entry in *The C. S. Lewis Readers'
Encyclopedia*, op. cit., p.81.
page 146: **'greatest English philosopher':** Jane O'Grady, *The Guardian*,
11 January 2001.
page 147: **'All that had happened':** A. N. Wilson, *C. S. Lewis: A Biography*
page 147: **Stella Adwinkle:** Hooper, *C. S. Lewis Companion & Guide*, pp.617–18.
page 148: **'On Obstinacy in Belief':** 'On Obstinacy in Belief', Richard A. Hill,
entry in *The C. S. Lewis Readers' Encyclopedia*, op. cit., p.304.
page 148: **'an inwardly optimistic':** *C. S. Lewis: A Biography*, rev. ed, Roger
Lancelyn Green and Walter Hooper, p.254.

SILVER CHAIR:
page 151: **'I fared onward':** *The Odyssey*, trans. by Samuel Butler
(London, 1900), Book 4.

JILL POLE:

page 154: **seven deadly sins:** 'Narnia and the Seven Deadly Sins' by Don W. King, first appeared in *Mythlore* 10 (Spring 1984), pp.14–19. Possible online resource: http://cslewis.drzeus.net/papers/7sins.html

page 155: **'reveals a Lewis':** Ford, *Companion to Narnia*

PRINCE RILIAN:

page 158: **'he's as good as an extra maid':** A. N. Wilson, op. cit., p.64.

THE LAST BATTLE

INTRODUCTION:

page 161: **Gili Bar-Hillel:** correspondence with author.

page 162: **Antichrist:** Hooper, *C. S. Lewis: A Companion & Guide*, p.426. See also 'Satan', Perry C. Bramlett, entry in *The C. S. Lewis Readers' Encyclopedia*, op. cit., p.361.

EMETH:

page 165: **'faithful':** Ford, *Companion to Narnia*, p.166. Lewis used the Hebrew term *emeth* in other works.

SHADOWLANDS:

page 171: **'way up':** 'The Golden Key', George MacDonald, *Dealing with the Fairies* (1867). Possible online resource: http://www.george-macdonald.com/golden_key.htm

AFTERWORD

page 177: **'a bullying weight':** *The Inklings*, p.222.

page 178: **muslims lie:** remarks about the Muslims can be found, among other places, in *Collected Letters of C. S. Lewis*, volume I, p.711. About Jews, also in various places but especially *Reflections on the Psalms*. 'For us the very name Jew is associated with finance, shopkeeping, money-lending and the like. This however, dates from the Middle Ages when Jews were not allowed to own land and were driven into occupations remote from the soil. Whatever characteristics the modern Jew has acquired from millennia of such occupations, they cannot have been those of his ancestors'. (*Reflections on the Psalms*, p.76). (Lewis accepts the stereotype, says it's encoded in Jewish culture – or perhaps even genes – but then thinks himself kind to Jews for saying corruption was forced upon them. Madness.) His views about Africans are clear from the 'brown girl' of 'the island' in *The Pilgrim's Regress*. In that allegory, she represents lust, and the hero hates her for making him succumb. He's later almost hypnotized by the sexual beat of an 'African tom-tom'. The hero is delighted when he finds 'at last . . . a girl with no trace of brown', which makes him feel a 'love so great and so pure' until he discovers she is 'only a brown girl' in disguise (*The Pilgrim's Regress*, pp.30–39). As one Lewis scholar says, it is 'most unfortunate' that 'the brown girls . . . grow darker the worse they are'. This may remind readers of Lewis's descriptions of the Calormenes, 'their white eyes flashing dreadfully in their brown faces' (*The Last Battle*, ch.3).

page 179: 'adult mind': *God in the Dock*, p.102.

page 179: 'polygamous Methodism': *Collected Letters of C. S. Lewis*, volume I, p.711.

page 179: 'abhorred': *Companion to Narnia*, p.345.

page 180: 'hostile': Wilson, p.137.

page 180: 'Lutheran': *The Inklings*, Humphrey Carpenter (London: Allen & Unwin, 1978) p.192.

page 181: 'Lewis's hatreds were petty': *The Natural History of Make-Believe*, John Goldthwaite (New York: Oxford University Press, 1996), p.228.

page 182: 'Like many Englishmen of his era': *Companion to Narnia*, p.95.

page 182: 'Orientals': Edward Said's *Orientalism* remains the starting point for anyone interested in exploring this aspect of racism. It's highly recommended.

page 182: 'Want of accuracy': Cromer, *Modern Egypt* (New York: Macmillan, 1908), p.168; quoted in Said, Edward, *Orientalism*, p.38. Said recommends Wilfrid Scawen Blunt's *Secret History of the English Occupation of Egypt* 'for a British view of British policy in Egypt that runs totally counter to Cromer's' (Said, p.354).

page 183: 'All the senses': *C. S. Lewis In Context*, Doris. T. Myers, pp.162–5.

page 183: 'One may well regret': *Reading With the Heart*, p.13.

page 186: 'Even as a fan': 'In Defense of C. S. Lewis', Gregg Easterbrook, *The Atlantic Monthly*, October 2001.

INDEX TO THE MAGICAL WORLDS OF NARNIA

About the Author

Formerly an editorial director of HarperCollins and a head writer of television's *Who Wants To Be a Millionaire?*, David Colbert is also the author of *The Magical Worlds of Harry Potter* and *The Magical Worlds of The Lord of the Rings* and the *Eyewitness* history series. A graduate of Brown University, he studied anthropology and mythology but spent most of his time reading randomly in the library, which is pretty much what he still does.